INVESTIGATING

CORPORATE FRAUD

BY INVESTIGATORS

Clyde A. Wilson and Chester P. Karrick, Jr.

Written By
    Chester P. Karrick, Jr.
    Third Edition

Copyright @ 2014 by Chester P. Karrick, Jr.
Copyright @ Revised March 2015 by Chester P. Karrick, Jr.
Copyright @ Revised April 2018 by Chester P. Karrick, Jr. 3rd edition

ISBN 9781984282316

All rights reserved. No part of this book may be used or reproduced by any means, graphic, electronic, or mechanical including photocopying, recording, taping or by any information storage retrieval system without the written permission of the author except in the case of brief quotations embodied in critical articles and reviews.

Authors Note: This book is a work covering 82 true corporate fraud investigation cases conducted by Private Investigators Clyde A. Wilson and Chester P. Karrick, Jr., the author. Clients and investigative suspects names are intentionally not disclosed to protect the rights of such companies and individuals.

The information included in this work is based solely on the remembrances and experiences of the author.

Copies of this book may be requested through Amazon.com or from the author as shown below.

Chester P. Karrick, Jr.
210 Garden Dr.
Friendswood, Texas 77546
cheskarr@yahoo.com

Thanks to Scott and Kim Zrubek for their assistance in cover design and computer layout for printing. Cover pictures pulled from Pixabay.com.

Self-published through Amazon's CreateSpace.

In Memory Of

CLYDE A. WILSON

1923 - 2008

ABOUT THE INVESTIGATORS

Clyde and Chester

This book covers a diverse sampling from over 400 true corporate investigations conducted by Clyde A. Wilson and the author, Chester Karrick, during the period 1969-1980.

Clyde Wilson was born in Houston in 1923 and moved to Austin as a young child after his father passed away. According to Clyde, he graduated from Bickler Elementary School in Austin. (I'm not sure such a school ever existed.) Clyde was drafted into the military in the early 1940's and fought in World War II. He was awarded two Purple Hearts and a Bronze Star.

Clyde's investigative training began in the military while serving in Morocco when assigned to investigate a series of thefts from local government supply warehouses. Based on the successful result from this assignment, Clyde was sent to Washington D. C. to attend various schools for investigative training including CID, CIA, and some of those other alphabet soup schools. As a result of this training, Clyde spent the rest of his military service infiltrating top government secret facilities to determine the effectiveness of their security. After the military, Clyde spent over a year as an insurance investigator. Bored with this endeavor, Clyde moved to Houston and opened his own investigative agency and remained in that business the balance of his working career spanning almost 40 years.

Some of Clyde's more notorious investigative cases involved the Moody Foundation Funds; Herman Estate Administrators; Ivana Trump in the divorce of Donald Trump; political slander case in 1970 involving a Houston Mayoral Candidate and a KTRK-TV Reporter; release of hostages in Ethiopia; Doris Day in a West Texas oil field swindle; West Texas ammonia storage tank fraud; Pilgrim Cleaners shotgun squad; and elected officials in Lufkin and Polk Counties. Clyde was among the top-notch detectives in Texas. He retired in the late 1990's as Houston's most celebrated and colorful private investigator.

Wilson passed away in November 2008 at the age of 85. A *Houston Chronicle* article quoted long time attorney friend David Burg, "Clyde Wilson can sweet-talk a confession out of a person when no police officer ever could." Although attorney "Race Horse" Haynes was often on the opposite side of Wilson on criminal cases, he came to respect the private investigator and said, "There will never be another Clyde Wilson."

Chester recalls an incident that Clyde related when he was on the witness stand during a court case when famous murder defense lawyer Percy Forman was grilling him. Percy was standing about three feet in front of Clyde, pointing a finger in Clyde's face and talking a mile a minute. He had Clyde really sweating. Clyde was trying to figure a way out. Interrupting Foreman, Clyde turned to the judge and asked if he might ask a question. The judge said, "Yes Clyde." Clyde asked, "Judge would you please ask Mr. Forman to stand back a couple more feet as his bad breath is about to make me sick?" Flustered, Foreman stepped back and said, "No more questions." Coincidentally, both were leaving the courthouse at the same time. Percy turned to Clyde and said, "Clyde, I thought we are friends." Clyde said, "We are friends Percy but you were about to eat my lunch up there on the stand. I had to figure a way out." It was always hard to get ahead of Clyde.

Chester graduated from Trinity University in San Antonio receiving a B.S. (how appropriate) Degree. He moved to Austin and attended the university while working full time for a local insurance company to cover his college costs. He received a Master's Degree in Professional Accounting in 1954 from the University of Texas. Chester joined a Houston oil and gas company upon graduation serving in several accounting management positions including controller of a chemical company and Assistant Director of Corporate Internal Audit.

Chester met Clyde Wilson when each of them worked on separate fraud cases at the oil and gas company where Chester was employed. The company engaged Clyde to investigate suspected fraud in cattle feed lot operations located in Nebraska and California. Based on the results of Clyde's investigation, Chester was requested to assist in preparing the fidelity insurance bond claim to recover the discovered $10,000,000 loss. (The first fraud case presented in this book.) At the same time Clyde investigated the cattle feed lot fraud, Chester was investigating a $125,000 forgery fraud involving company purchase orders.

After those investigations were competed, the company saw the need for two full time company investigators to investigate possible frauds in its businesses served by over 130,000 employees. Clyde was hired as a full time Security Consultant reporting to the company CEO with Chester designated to assist Clyde.

The company CEO notified company division presidents that starting that day all prior possible illegal activities not previously discovered were forgiven but from that day forward anyone caught involved in fraudulent activities would be prosecuted with no exceptions. All company personnel were advised that anyone suspecting fraud would notify Chester who would protect the source and organize with Clyde an investigation of the suspected area. Thus, together they began a ten-year span of fraud investigations.

INTRODUCTION

While Chester sat on the porch facing the lake with a good book in his lap, the rain was coming down in sheets with the weatherman forecasting nothing but rain for the next six days. *No golf this week*! Knowing he would be very bored before the week would be over, Chester tried to think of something that he could do during the week of bad weather. Having traveled as an auditor and private investigator with Clyde Wilson for seven years conducting investigations for a public company and then as partner with Clyde Wilson in their firm Wilson & Carrick Investigations, Chester thought back about their work and realized that information about their criminal investigative cases was never shared with his wife and daughter. They had no idea of the type of work that was performed away from home each week. The idea surfaced that a book could be written to explain the reason why so much time was spent on the road giving examples of their work. Thus the result is this book titled "Investigating Corporate Fraud."

Chester selected 82 of the most representative true corporate investigation cases and audits for this book out of the over 400 cases conducted at a Houston oil and gas corporation with over 130,000 employees and after that at their investigative firm, Wilson & Carrick Investigations.

These true crime investigative cases show how various frauds, embezzlements and thefts can be detected by using resources including employees, vengeful letters, third party tips, records, physical observations, and a lot of luck. These cases cover true investigations conducted in the majority of the Continental United States, Mexico, Canada, Caribbean, and the Middle East.

Cases in the book are grouped under the business headings of Foreign; Shipbuilding; Pipelines, Oil and Gas, Convenience Stores; Insurance; Real Estate; Agriculture and Construction Equipment; Banking; Automotive Parts and Equipment; Chemicals, Paper Products, Mining; Farming and Produce; and Miscellaneous.

In many of the cases management had become more concerned with matters at the country club and business organizations that "no one was watching the store." I cannot emphasize enough how necessary it is for staff management to make appearances and reviews of field operations, talking to production employees about any irregularities suspected, review employee's standard of living, and specific attention to areas that lack proper internal controls for possible fraud. **Opportunity is a major motivator for Greed!**

Chester had no training in the techniques of investigating and interrogating fraud suspects. This included taking proper statements designed to provide documentation to facilitate prosecution of applicable persons and recovery of monies lost. Clyde proved to be a good instructor as Chester developed many of the techniques used in fraud investigations from Clyde. Chester's background in accounting was very useful in the preparation of fidelity insurance bond claims to recover losses due to fraud.

During the ten years they worked together, Clyde and Chester conducted over 400 investigations and security reviews that resulted in the termination and conviction of many client employees, suppliers, and contractors. In addition, fraud of over $40,000,000 was uncovered with recoveries from employees, third parties, and fidelity bond insurance claims of over $30,000,000. Cost savings from security and internal reviews resulted in subsequent savings of over $ 10,000,000. Their motto was that the first three words of the Investigators Bible are "**Get The Money**."

We were primarily concerned with identifying the guilty individuals, recovering the losses through restitution and/or fidelity bond insurance claims, and pursuing prosecution of the guilty.

Many of these fraud cases seemed substantial during the period 1969 to 1980 but today you are considered a piker if the fraud doesn't amount to at least a billion dollars.

In Texas, at the time of our investigations in 1969-1980, Private Investigators were licensed by the state but held no police power nor bore the intimidating powers of the police uniform, no side arm and badge, nor threats of being taken to the police station for interrogation.

The investigator can invite a suspect into a room for an interview, however, the suspect is under no obligation to stay nor can the investigator detain him. Each suspect could refuse to talk to us and leave at any time. We never had any one walk. On one occasion a suspect told us he was leaving but never got past the doorknob before returning. We solved fraud based on our wits and imagination.

When we were in a room of several employees from the area we suspected fraud, Clyde would nudge me when he identified persons he thought were probably involved. He said the hair on the back of his head would stand up when he looked at someone he thought guilty or with knowledge of possible fraud. When I decided on my suspect, we accompanied them to private meeting rooms for interrogation. In nearly all cases we were right. Clyde had a glass eye as a result of a domestic accident. At times when interrogations were not proceeding as planned, he would pop his glass eye out and spin it on the table. Confessions were usually then expedited, as they wanted out of there. Clyde was one of the best interrogators of suspects. Clyde had an enormous amount of common sense that was very helpful in interrogations.

Their investigative firm Wilson & Carrick Investigations was established in 1977. Clients were primarily oil and gas companies, law firms, financial institutions and industrial companies. They never worked domestic or undercover assignments.

After several years together, Chester decided to retire. However, they continued to be involved in several other business ventures.

TABLE OF CONTENTS

CLYDE AND CHESTER MEET 1
    THE CATTLE RUSTLERS 3
    THE FORGERY 9

FOREIGN 13
    THE MEXICAN JAILBIRD 15
    DON'T CROSS THE BORDER 29
    BEWARE THE CON MAN 33
    STORE SITE ACQUISITIONS 37
    ACCUSING THE ACCUSER 39
    THE ONE THAT GOT AWAY 43
    THE MEXICAN SCARE 47
    BERMUDA CASH FLOW 49
    BEWARE THE CANADIAN JAILHOUSE 51

SHIPBUILDING 53
    PAINT AND LEAD CAPER 55
    OVER THE FENCE THEY WILL GO 57
    THE BEACH HOUSE 61
    THE TRAVELING LUGGAGE 65
    THE DIRTY DEAL 67

PIPELINES, OIL AND GAS, CONVENIENCE STORES 71
    THE CRUDE OIL AND THE DEEP FREEZE CASE 73
    THE ROSE AND THE PAPER SACK 77
    EQUIPPING THE RANCH 81
    THE STOLEN OFFICE EQUIPMENT AND DRUGS 83
    WHO GOT THE ROYALTIES? 85
    PISTOL IN THE SKY 87
    THE STOLEN MAPS 91
    THE BUGS 93

INSURANCE 95
    THE INSURANCE SCAM 97

REAL ESTATE 99
    THE SAFE DEPOSIT BOX 101
    MISUSING THE COMPANY LABOR 103
    THE GUARD WHO SHOT STRAIGHT 105
    WHAT HAPPENED TO THE RENT? 109

AGRICULTURE AND CONSTRUCTION EQUIPMENT 111
    THE DISAPPEARING BATTERIES 113
    KICKING BACK 117
    FALSE BANK DEPOSITS 121
    OUT OF TRUST 123
    CREDIT AND COLLECTIONS 127
    CONVERSION OF CUSTOMER'S PAYMENTS 129

BANKING 131
    THE VOID CERTIFICATES OF DEPOSIT 133
    THE PHONY BANK LOANS 135
    HIDDEN ASSETS 139

TABLE OF CONTENTS (CONT'D.)

BILKING THE BANK	141
USING THE BANK AS A FICTITIOUS PAYEE	145
TRUSTING THE TRUST OFFICER	147
TAKING A STATEMENT	149

AUTOMOTIVE PARTS AND EQUIPMENT **153**

HORSE BARNS AND FENCES	155
DISAPPEARING TAIL PIPES	157
THE FICTITIOUS COMPANY	159
MISSISSIPPI MUD	161
AUTOMOBILE KICKBACKS	163
THE NARROW ESCAPE	165
UNDERCOVER IN MISSISSIPPI	169
CHASING THE HORSES	171
THE MISSING PARTS	173

CHEMICALS, PAPER PRODUCTS, MINING **175**

THE VENGEFUL LETTER	177
THE STRIKING EXPERIENCE	183
CORNED BEEF AND CABBAGE	185
PINE STUMP SHORTAGES	189
THE STRAYING MATTRESSES	191
STAY AWAY FROM THE FIREWATER	193
SUSPECTED NAVAL STORES FRAUD	195
THE COURTHOUSE SETUP	197
THE UNDERCOVER MAN	199
THE BOMB THREAT	203
ONE COAL NIGHT	205
COLD COAL REVIEW	207

FARMING AND PRODUCE **209**

SEX AND THE LAND DEALS	211
CLIPPING THE CO-OP	213
THE GRAPE WARS	215
FARMING AND AGRICULTURE NOTES RECEIVABLE	217
TAMPERING WITH THE SCALES	219

MISCELLANEOUS **221**

AN EYE FOR A WATCH	223
OUTFOXING THE FOX	225
THE PRE-EMPLOYEMENT PHYSICAL	227
THE LOBBYIST	229
WHAT HAPPENED TO THE STOCK?	231
STOLEN LADIES PURSES	233
CROSSING AGAINST THE LIGHT	235
THE TUGBOAT COLLISION	237
UNAUTHORIZED TRIP	239
PREVENTING ASSAULT ON A CELEBERITY	241
SECURING $ 1,000,000 IN CASH	243
CROSS-DRESSED ATTORNEY	245
THE BOTCHED EMPLOYEMENT SEARCH	247

CLYDE AND CHESTER MEET

Investigating Corporate Fraud

THE CATTLE RUSTLERS

The company had recently acquired a major corporation that primarily engaged in oil and gas exploration and production, irrigation farms, two cattle feedlots, and ranching.

A minor area of activity of the acquired company involved operating two cattle feedlots, one in mid American and the other in the West. Each feedlot operation generally involved feeding about 10,000 head of cattle.

About two months after the corporation was acquired, the parent company CEO received a telephone call from the head of a major corporation with other business interests in the area of the feedlot operations. This individual advised the CEO that he might want to take a look at the feedlot operations.

This was very non-specific information but the executive thought that this information was worth pursuing.

At this time one of the big five public accounting firms was auditing the feedlot operations, starting with counting all the cattle in the various pens. This same accounting firm had audited the feedlot operations each year for the past five years. They had not noted any irregularities in the past.

The company CEO called Clyde to come to his office. Clyde was told of the telephone call and suggested that a review of the feedlot operations might be in order. (At this time Clyde was operating from his Private Investigative Firm.
He had not yet been hired as a full time Security Consultant for the company.
Also, Clyde and Chester were not yet working together at this time.)

As the information was very non-specific, the executive wanted Clyde to take a look at the mid American feedlot operation. Clyde was told to dress up in a blue pinstriped suit and conservative tie so that he would look like an auditor. The executive wanted Clyde to join the public accounting auditors and assist in the cattle count. Clyde was told, "I do not want you talking to people or nosing around. Just count the cattle with the auditors and see what you can overhear about this operation. Understood?"

Clyde agreed and left for the feedlot as requested.

Clyde arrived at the feedlot about 7am the next morning. It was midwinter and the outside temperature was near zero. The cattle were thigh deep in snow and mud. Clyde thought there was no way he was going to wade out into those cattle pens and count cattle all day. He thought that the cattle probably would be moved around in the pens that night by feedlot employees and he would be counting the same cattle the next day.

The Cattle Rustlers

Trying to figure a way out of this predicament, fortunately a feedlot employee arrived early on the scene. The employee was a young man about 22 years old. Clyde struck up a conversation with the young man who advised he had been working at the feedlot a little more that a year. As the young man's last name was the same as a world famous man, Clyde asked if he was related. The young man stated that the well-known gentleman was his uncle.

Clyde, sensing an opportunity to perhaps bring any improper feedlot activity to an early conclusion, advised the young man, "I'm an investigator for the company out of Houston. I know all about the thefts and fraud going on at the feedlots. I am going to put everyone that works here in jail. I am going to give the first person that confirms my findings a free ride. If you want to tell me everything, you will be the first person given the chance for the free ride. Otherwise, you will also be going to jail."

The young man began to cry and said he could not go to jail, as it would be a great embarrassment to his family. He could not stand that thought. He told Clyde that although he had been employed at the feedlot only a little over a year, he knew everything that was going on and he would tell him anything he wanted to know saying, "Please do not send me to jail."

Clyde, freezing cold from being outside in the weather, told the young man, "Fine let's you and me get out of the cold and go downtown to a nice warm restaurant, get some coffee, and talk about the situation."

Over several cups of coffee, the feedlot employee told Clyde in detail about all the frauds perpetrated at the feedlot operation.

Among the many irregularities described to Clyde, were falsified death certificates for cattle, payments to suppliers for feed billed but not delivered, payments to veterinarians for unperformed services and unsupplied drugs, dummy future sales contracts, and falsification of sales prices on company cattle sold.

Clyde was advised that there were an unusual number of cattle death certificates prepared to falsify the deaths of cattle. The cattle were subsequently sold and the monies split among the employees. Clyde asked what the auditors were told about disposition of the dead cattle carcasses. They were told there was a local zoo that received the carcasses to feed the lions.

Clyde later went to the zoo and found only one toothless lion that couldn't even chew any meat.

The feedlot employees had a deal with a local feed store for invoices to be submitted covering overpriced feed deliveries that were never delivered. The monies derived from this fraud were split between the employees and the feed store operator.

The feedlot employees also had a deal with a local veterinarian to invoice for services and drugs which were never provided. The vet also overcharged for actual services and drugs provided. The feedlot employees and vet split the monies received from this fraud.

In cattle feedlot operations, like this one, young calves are brought to the feedlot in early spring, fattened, and then sold in the fall. Hopefully a profit would be realized when the cattle were sold, resulting from the difference in the cattle acquisition costs, feed costs and vet services than the sales price. The company as well as outsiders owned the cattle fed at the feedlot.

Feedlot employees generated future cattle sales contracts through one of their fictitious companies with the sale being programmed for the fall. Such contracts were not reflected on the feedlot books. If prices for cattle were high, resulting in a profit, the sale was reflected in a way on the books that the employees through their fictitious companies realized the profits. If cattle prices were low, resulting in a loss, the contracts were torn up and the loss suffered from such cattle sales were borne by the company.

In other cattle sales, the employees would falsify the sales invoices to understate sales prices and retain the different between the understated sales price and the actual sales price for themselves.

In addition, there were other lesser scams perpetrated.

All of this information was reduced to a detailed written statement and signed by the employee before noon.

Clyde telephoned the CEO to advise of his findings. The CEO proceeded to cuss and berate Clyde and he said, "I told you to go out there and count cattle and you did not do what I told you." After the tirade, the man laughed, "I knew you would not follow my instructions and would go off on your own as you always do."

Clyde was advised that the CEO was going to contact the public accounting firm and state that all this fraud had occurred under their watch and that they were going to have to clean this mess up at no cost to the company. The public accounting firm was also advised that Clyde was being sent to the West coast to investigate that feedlot operation as the same frauds were probably occurring there as employees have been rotated between the two operations.

As the former owner had carried a fidelity insurance bond on its employees, a fidelity bond claim would be filed upon final determination of the loss.

In the meantime, Clyde worked with the local authorities to prosecute the feedlot employees with the exception of the young man who provided all the information.

The Cattle Rustlers

While the auditors were reconstructing the loss, which had occurred over the past several years, Clyde headed to the West coast feedlot, which was almost a duplicate of the other feedlot operation.

During the next several days, Clyde interrogated and took signed statements from the feedlot employees, which set forth the same fraudulent activities over the same time frame as the mid-American feedlot.

Clyde was advised to prosecute these feedlot employees, as applicable.

Clyde put together a package containing the statements of the feedlot employees together with a summary of the losses for presentation to the local district attorney.

The district attorney, who was campaigning for re-election, reviewed the files and told Clyde the employees' activities did not constitute prosecutorial offenses.

Clyde knew that this was not true but after further discussions was not able to change the district attorney's position.

Clyde left the district attorney's office and pondered his next move.

There were two local newspapers, the largest a liberal publication, while the other, a smaller newspaper owned and operated by a caustic local that did not cater to advertisers or the city's elite but called all the shots as he saw it no matter whom he offended.

Clyde decided to approach the editor (and owner) of the small local newspaper. Clyde asked the owner, "What is the story on your local district attorney?"

The editor told Clyde, "The DA is a local boy that does not like to try cases and is afraid to indict unless it is a gut cinch. The DA hangs out at the local country club and golf course with the local elite and likes to be treated as one of the good ole boys."

Clyde told the newspaper editor about his investigation of the local feedlot operation and at the other feedlot. He also told the editor that the local DA refused to prosecute. He gave the editor his file.

The editor advised Clyde that if he had the evidence of the frauds he had just described, he would be glad to take on the DA and the establishment about this matter. He also advised Clyde that the DA was buddies at the country club with many of the feedlot employees that had allegedly perpetrated these frauds. He told Clyde to come back in the morning to give him time to review the file.

The next day when Clyde returned to the newspaper office, the editor advised Clyde, "You have all the evidence you told me about and we are going to see that the DA prosecutes these cases."

Over the next couple of days, the editor published various aspects of the investigation and questioned why the DA did not have the guts to prosecute.

After several days of being chastised in the newspaper, the DA called Clyde to come to his office. Upon arrival the DA advised Clyde that he had changed his mind and decided to prosecute the cases after all.

The various feedlot employees were successfully prosecuted but the newspaper articles had done their damage, as the DA did not get re-elected.

Back home, Chester was working with the public accounting firm on improving internal controls in the feedlot operations and determining the feedlot loss.

Upon completion of the audit review, the loss approached $10 million dollars and an appropriate fidelity insurance bond claim was filed and collected. It was during calculations of this loss that Chester met Clyde.

Not much later the company sold the feedlot operations, as they did not fit with other company operations.

THE FORGERY

When auditors observed that the cost of the company's office supplies had increased by over 100 % in the past six months, Chester was asked to review the purchases.

Beginning the review, Chester studied the company's purchasing procedures and internal controls.

A purchase order was issued to purchase the office supplies, then approved and signed by a designated purchasing agent. Orders were received at the loading docks in the basement of the company's office building. A clerk in the receiving area signed the packing slip that accompanied the shipment to certify receipt of the items shown.

A supervisor in the purchasing department later completed and signed a receiving report covering supplies received based on receipt of the approved packing slip. He then attached the packing slip to the receiving report and forwarded the paper work to the accounting department.

When the supplier invoice reached accounting, it was matched to the appropriate purchase order and receiving report. A check was then cut to pay for the purchase. Internal controls for the purchases appeared adequate.

In reviewing the invoices covering supplies purchased during the past six months, Chester noted that the same purchasing agent was ordering all of these purchases. Most office supply purchases were being made from the same supplier company.

Further review disclosed no purchases had been made from this supplier prior to the last six months.

Chester then checked office supply purchases for the prior twelve months. He noted that purchases during the last six months were $125,000 over the average purchases for the prior six-month period.

Chester checked all of the related purchase orders, packing slips, receiving reports and invoices covering purchases from the new supplier. All signatures and approvals appeared to be proper.

Taking several of the purchase orders to the originating purchasing agent, Chester asked him about the purchases.

The purchasing agent looked at his signature on the purchase orders a long time.

He then turned to Chester and said, "That's my signature but I don't remember ordering any supplies from this company. I don't even know anyone working there."

The Forgery

Chester thought this was strange. Thinking about the other personnel in the purchasing department. Chester recalled a conversation overhead at coffee one day.

Another purchasing agent made a statement to a person at the table. "Sign your name on this paper and within five minutes I can sign your name better than you can."

This same purchasing agent was known to sport several good looking girls around town as he always seemed to have a large roll of money to spend. He always claimed his grandmother had left him a lot of money.

Since the purchasing agent told Chester he didn't order the supplies, Chester went to the receiving area and sought out the clerk who had signed the packing slips covering the receipt of the office supplies.

The clerk was shown the paper work with his name on it. He studied the Packing Slips.

He then turned to Chester and said, "That's my signature but I didn't receive any of those shipments."

The clerk and Chester then took a quick inventory of office supplies and found substantial shortages. They speculated that supplies ordered from the new supplier were never received.

As Chester surmised that a forger was at work in defrauding the company he requested that Clyde Wilson be engaged to pursue his findings.

Clyde advised Chester to get signatures and handwriting samples from the receiving clerk and the purchasing agent whose name appeared on the purchase order.

Clyde also suggested that Chester obtain handwriting samples from the purchasing agent that Chester suspected of forgery.

After Chester got the appropriate handwriting samples, Clyde called in a handwriting forgery expert from the local police department.

When the handwriting expert finished his review, he advised Clyde that he believed the suspect had signed all of the documents covering the office supply purchases in question. He stated, however, that the forgeries were so perfect he could not testify conclusively in court that our suspect signed the documents.

Clyde felt that it was time to call on the owner of the office supply company. He went to the firm and asked to speak to the owner.

Clyde confronted the owner with our suspicions that he was giving kickbacks to our client's purchasing agent.

Further, Clyde told the owner no supply deliveries were being made from his company to the client.

The owner was then told that the information gathered was going to be presented to the district attorney with a request for a Grand Jury investigation.

The owner stated he didn't want to be any part of a Grand Jury investigation. The owner then admitted that he and the company's purchasing agent had a deal, whereby they split 50/50 all the monies received from the fraudulent purchase orders. He also admitted that no supplies were ever delivered.

Clyde always had a saying, "The first three words of the investigators Bible are 'Get The Money'."

Accordingly, Clyde made a deal with the owner.

Clyde agreed not to pursue prosecuting the owner if the company was reimbursed $125,342.42 covering the fraudulent activity. The owner agreed.

Clyde obtained a signed statement from the owner covering his part in the fraud and the involvement with the company's purchasing agent so that prosecution of the employee could be pursued.

Returning to the office, the purchasing agent was called into the office by Clyde and shown a copy of the statement taken from the office supply company owner.

The purchasing agent broke down and confessed to his part in the fraud including forging the signatures on the applicable documents. Clyde then obtained a signed statement from the employee covering his role in the fraud. The employee was then terminated.

The statements were turned over to the district attorney's office. The purchasing agent was prosecuted and convicted. The company's loss had been recovered.

FOREIGN

Investigating Corporate Fraud

THE MEXICAN JAILBIRD

While attending an auditing/security seminar at Lake Geneva, Clyde and Chester received a telephone call requesting them to check out a chemical company headquartered in Mexico City that was a part of a New York City operating division. The operation in Mexico City had begun to have considerable losses during the last several months.

They agreed to leave for Mexico the next day.

Two employees from the New York office agreed to meet them in Mexico City. A vice president responsible for the Mexican Division operation and a division auditor from the New York office met them in Mexico City the following day.

They could not pin point any specific problem other than during the past couple of months the operation had suddenly started to experience large losses.

The company was engaged in the sale of various agricultural chemical products throughout Mexico that were being purchased from Mexican manufacturers for resale.

These business operations were conducted through a Mexican subsidiary company managed locally by a general manager who had considerable authority to act on behalf of the client.

His duties involved sales, credit and collection, purchases, inventory control, treasury, accounting and other areas.

After several years of operation, the U. S. parent company decided to discontinue the Mexican operations at year-end.

The general manager was advised of this decision. He was requested to slowly liquidate the company over the next six months. He was assured that he would be transferred into an equivalent assignment in the United States when operations were closed.

He was advised to proceed to collect all accounts receivable and attempt to dispose of all inventories by year-end, even if such sales were at cost.

The general manager was the only employee in the Mexican office to be told about the plan to discontinue company operations at year-end.

The vice president in New York responsible for the Mexican operation came to Mexico City to check on the operation every three months. Chester found out later that the general manager had conned the vice president on each occasion to go to Acapulco or Puerto Vallarta so that the vice president never saw the other employees or looked at the company books. However, the vice president had become suspicious when the operation started incurring operating losses.

Clyde and Chester arrived at the Mexico City office to learn that the general manager (we will call him Jose, not his real name) had unexpectedly resigned the past Friday.

Jose was scheduled to come to the office in a few minutes after they arrived to collect his last paycheck.

They decided to interview Jose when he arrived in hopes of getting a handle on whatever was contributing to the client's losses including the possibility of fraud.

Neither Clyde nor Chester could speak Spanish. Chester could read enough Spanish to get the main idea of what was written.

Suspicious, since Jose had resigned so suddenly, Chester began interviewing other office employees through a bilingual office secretary.

These interviews were difficult, as Chester could not always tell if the secretary was translating to English exactly what the employees were saying.

It was also obvious that either no one was aware of a possible fraud or that they just did not want to get involved.

In the meantime, Jose had arrived and Clyde began the interview.

Jose was a highly educated man having earned a doctorate degree from a university in the United States. He was a Mexican native but spoke excellent English.

Jose was about six feet six inches tall and weighed 250 pounds. He dressed impeccably and obviously enjoyed a very high standard of living. He lived with his wife and five children in a private residence in Mexico City.

Initially, Clyde was unable to gain any information relative to any financial problems at the client's operation.

Clyde came back and forth to Chester asking, "Have you got any questions I can ask him? What have you found out? I'm running out of anything to talk about!"

About an hour had gone by and Chester was not having any luck either.

In a few minutes the assistant general manager arrived in the office and Chester tried gaining information from him.

Investigating Corporate Fraud

The man grew very excited and Chester could not make heads or tails out of what he was saying. The secretary couldn't seem to keep up with the conversation.

Finally, the secretary said the assistant general manager didn't want to talk to Chester, as he was afraid that he would lose his job.

Chester told the secretary to tell him, "Don't worry, if you don't talk to me you are going to lose your job right now!"

Chester told the secretary to calm the assistant general manager and to slowly explain that he suspected his former boss of stealing from the company.

Taking a stab in the dark, Chester told the Secretary, "Ask him what he knows about his former boss's thefts!"

The secretary and the assistant general manager jabbered back and forth with Chester not understanding anything that was said.

Finally as a last resort, Chester asked the secretary to type in English what the man had said.

After what seemed like hours (but only was a few minutes), the secretary handed Chester a typed half page. The translation stated that the assistant general manager had found out the past week that the company had received a station wagon from a customer in partial payment on an account receivable. Jose had taken the station wagon home and later taken the station wagon title to the courthouse and transferred ownership into his name. He had stolen the station wagon from the company.

Chester quickly passed a note to Clyde covering this information.

After further interrogation, Jose finally admitted to having stolen the station wagon. He gave Clyde a signed statement acknowledging this theft. He swore that he was not involved in any other fraudulent activities.

Knowing full well that they had probably only hit the tip of the iceberg, they had no way to detain the former general manager any longer at the office.

A little latter, they met with the vice-president and auditor who had arrived from the New York office.

They did not know that Jose had resigned. They were shown the statement Clyde had just obtained.

Based on the statement, it was felt that they should go to the company's corporate attorney in Mexico City to learn their options, including, how they could proceed with possible prosecution of the former general manager. If they could have him jailed for stealing the station wagon, information relative to other frauds could probably be obtained.

After making copies of the former general manager's statement, the original was left in the attorney's security vault.

After dinner that night, Clyde, Chester, and the two New York representatives headed to their hotel rooms.

Lagging back, Clyde turned to Chester and said, "You know that Jose isn't stupid. When he gets home and thinks about that statement he will realize that the statement is the only thing we have on him. He's going to get a couple of goons to come to our hotel room tonight and try to get it back. Let's wait until these guys get upstairs and then we will check out of here and check into another hotel down the street."

The next morning when they arrived at the New Yorker's hotel to meet for breakfast, they found the two men standing by the hotel front door with their bags packed.

Chester asked, "Where are you going? You just got here."

The vice-president replied, "We are going home. You stay here and finish up the investigation any way you want. We're through!"

Clyde asked, "What happened?"

The New Yorkers related, "About 2:00 am last night, two big Mexican men broke into our room and began searching through our baggage. Then they searched the room looking for the statement taken from the former general manager. We crawled under the bed and hollered, Help! Police! But no one came to our rescue."

The Mexicans had taken their time going through their room and, not finding anything, left.

The New Yorkers then asked, "Didn't they break into your rooms too?"

They replied, "No, we didn't hear anyone outside or in our rooms."

They didn't admit that they had moved to another hotel.

Being scared to death, the New Yorkers had stayed up the rest of the night, packed their bags, and after telling Clyde and Chester what had happened, were headed for home.

That morning Clyde and Chester went back to the company's office. Chester began going through the accounting records. In a little while Chester discovered that accounts receivable for two new customers, unknown to the office staff, had grown to over $300,000 over the past several months. After further review, he concluded that the former general manager owned the two companies.

Chester went to the central courthouse in Mexico City to review the corporate register that contained corporate names, incorporators, addresses, and registered agents.

By mid-morning he located the two companies in question in the courthouse records. Not surprisingly, the name of the incorporator and registered agent was the former general manager. Chester made copies of these documents.

Tracing the address of the companies, Chester found that the location was a private office Jose had leased in another part of town. The office was located on the tenth floor at the top of a local office building.

Through further interviews with the client's Mexican office employees, Chester pieced together the story that Jose had told someone of his plan to go into business to compete against the company. When he had become established he would quit the company. He had bragged that he would put the client out of business. Jose had not told anyone that the client was going to shut down the business at year-end.

He discovered Jose had organized the two competing companies during the past year. Obviously, he had not disclosed this fact to his New York employer. Jose's brother operated these companies in the other office building under the ex-employee's direction.

This office was also used by Jose to entertain young women every evening with lavish parties. Such parties required a lot of cash that was being diverted from his employer.

Jose had extended credit, made loans, and consigned the client's inventory to his personal companies concealing his activities on his employer's books.

Further review disclosed that Jose had sent telegrams to all of the company's consignment warehouses advising that title to all company products should be transferred to another company, that was one of those Jose owned. He in effect had stolen his employer's entire inventory.

During the last several months when company sales were made to large customers, Jose transmitted his company invoice to the customer. The customer was advised that the company invoicing was a subsidiary company of his employer. He justified this action by saying that the invoices were being handled this way for tax purposes. The company's books reflected that the sale was made to one of the former employee's companies.

When the customer paid the invoice, the money went to one of Jose's companies at his personal office.

On the company books he made an entry showing the sale as being made to one of his personal companies that never paid any of the invoices. This procedure had been followed until over $300,000 had built up in accounts receivable that had been siphoned out of the Company.

At this point, Chester calculated the total loss to the client as being over $1,000,000.

Chester related his findings to Clyde.

Clyde felt that it was now time to find a good criminal attorney in Mexico City. Without putting Jose in jail, Clyde and Chester knew they would not get any more information from him.

Not knowing any criminal lawyers in the city, they decided to bring a TV personality from Texas to Mexico City to gain an introduction to the U. S. Ambassador to Mexico. Clyde felt the Ambassador could refer them to a good Mexican criminal attorney. Clyde knew the TV personality had worked with the Ambassador previously.

A couple of days later they accompanied the TV personality to the Ambassador's office.

The TV personality began telling the Ambassador that he was bringing Mexican prisoners from Texas to Mexico next week for exchange of American prisoners to be returned to Texas. He wanted to take TV pictures of the exchange in the Ambassador's office.

The Ambassador advised, "You may bring your TV cameras and take all the pictures you want, but neither I nor my staff will be here."

The Ambassador then turned to Chester and asked, "Are you folks with him?"

Chester replied, "I've never seen the SOB before in my life."

The ambassador said, "Good, come on into my office."

Based on the recommendation of the ambassador, a criminal attorney was retained.

After reviewing the case to date with the attorney, they went with the attorney to the office of the Attorney General of Mexico City.

The criminal lawyer was a bi-linguist. The Attorney General advised that he did not speak nor understand English.

Clyde related to the criminal attorney information he wanted conveyed to the Attorney General about the fraud at their client's office including the statement taken from the former employee. The Attorney General did not seem to understand the attorney's presentations.

Clyde told the criminal attorney about three times to convey exactly the words he was giving him. Still he got no reaction.

Finally, Clyde told the criminal attorney if he didn't convey his exact words he was going to knock him on his behind. The lawyer spoke for a while. Still he got no reaction.

Clyde hauled off and knocked the lawyer over the sofa and onto the floor.

Chester blurted out, "Oh No! We will be the only ones going to jail."

But surprisingly, the Attorney General got up out of his chair and came around the desk, smiled, and stuck out his hand to shake hands. He then started speaking in English. He said he understood our problem and asked how he could help.

It was obvious that the Attorney General did not like the criminal attorney we had hired so he was quickly dismissed.

The Attorney General read the statement Clyde had taken from Jose and questioned Chester about the other information he had found.

He said, "You don't need a criminal lawyer. If you want your former general manager picked up and put in jail, I'll have that accomplished before late afternoon."

Based on the reputation of the Mexican jails, Clyde and Chester knew that after Jose spent some time in jail, he would be cooperative the next time they talked to him.

By that night Jose was in jail in a cell with 15 other prisoners, all sleeping in bunk beds stacked four bunks high. Conditions in the jail were horrible. There were no mattresses, pillows, sheets, blankets, etc. provided. The jailed had to pay for any of these conveniences including decent meals. Being a Mexican aristocrat, the other prisoners hated him as much if not more than they would a gringo.

Over the next few days, Jose was able to obtain money from his family to buy his way into a cell with only three others. He was also able to buy a mattress, blankets, pillows and eatable food. Food normally served in the jail was absolutely nauseating.

At that time in Mexico, a person could be picked up and placed in jail for a year without being formally charged.

Mexican Jailbird

Going into jail, the six foot six inch man weighed about 250 pounds. Visiting with him a few months later, the man was a nervous wreck and had lost more than 70 pounds.

Clyde and Chester knew that Jose would try to find ways to intimidate them even though he was in jail. Neither had a permit to work in Mexico.

A day or so later they happened to be in their hotel lobby around noon. The hotel clerk told Clyde he had a telephone call that he then transferred to the house phone.

Answering the phone, the caller identified himself as being the Chief of Police of Mexico City.

The Chief told Clyde, "I'm sending a police car to the hotel to get you and Chester."

The company airplane that had brought them to Mexico City was at the Mexico City private air terminal. The plane was left there to bring them home when ready.

Clyde shouted to Chester, "Pack the bags, pay the bills, get a taxi and call the pilots. We are leaving the airport in about fifteen minutes. Tell the pilots to file their flight plan and be ready at the end of the runway when we get there. We will take off immediately."

It was obvious to Clyde that they had been turned in to the police for not having a work permit.

Continuing on the telephone, Clyde then told the Chief, "I appreciate your invitation to visit your jail. I have heard many good things about you and your jail facilities. But we won't be able to visit with you this trip. I'll call you when we come back and we can get together then."

The Chief said, "Senor, you don't understand. Wait there now for the police car to pick you up."

Clyde replied, "Thanks again for the invitation, but we just don't have time this trip to visit with you. We'll call you when we come back in a few weeks." Clyde then hung up the telephone.

By this time, Chester had packed the bags, paid the hotel bills, called the pilots at the airport, and hailed a taxi. They jumped in the taxi. After they had gone about a block they heard police sirens. Looking back, they saw three police cars stop in front of the hotel.

The taxi driver was told to drive to the private airport terminal located on the opposite side of the runways from the main commercial Mexico City airport.

Just as they boarded the airplane, they saw several police cars coming from the commercial airport with lights flashing and sirens blaring, crossing the active runways, and coming towards their airplane.

Chester hollered at the pilots, "Give her the gas, and let's get out of here NOW!"

The airplane roared down the runway becoming airborne just over the top of the police cars. Another close escape!

During the investigation, Clyde and Chester went back home several times to pursue other frauds. Leaving Jose in jail for a while longer would loosen his tongue the next time around.

They returned to Mexico City a couple of weeks later in one of the company's Jet Star airplanes. At about a thousand feet and a quarter to a half-mile out from the landing runway, all power in the airplane went out. Without the jet engines, the airplane came down almost like a rock right onto an active runway for departing airplanes. Their airplane barely missed a couple of airplanes just becoming airborne.

They were scared to death.

Chester asked the pilots, "What happened?"

The pilots replied, "When you come in from the mountains like we did sometimes you lose power due to the high altitude."

This certainly didn't seem like a logical answer, but they decided not to pursue the matter any further.

Each time they returned to Mexico City and stayed in the El Presidente Hotel there would be a basket of flowers in Clyde's room and a basket of fresh fruit in Chester's room.

They were in Chester's room discussing what they were going to do next on the case when they heard organ music coming from the sidewalk area eight floors below. Looking out the window, they saw an organ grinder with a monkey on a leash holding a tin cup.

The monkey looked up and waved at Clyde and Chester.

Clyde told Chester, "Throw the monkey some money."

Chester threw some paper pesos out the window but the wind caught them and blew them away.

"Throw him some coins," said Clyde.

Chester threw several peso coins out the window but they hit the sidewalk next to the monkey and bounced away.

Clyde said, "Here let me show you." Clyde picked up a big orange and threw it out the window.

The monkey looked up with his arms outstretched but the orange hit him square on top of the head and he went down like a ton of bricks.

Chester hollered at Clyde, "I think you killed him. Let's get out of here before that organ grinder comes after us."

They ran down the hall, rode the elevator down to the lobby, ran across the lobby and sat down on the sofas away from the front door.

In a minute, the organ grinder came in the door dragging the dead monkey behind. He was yelling at the top of his voice.

Of course Clyde and Chester couldn't understand what he was saying. The organ grinder got in the elevator and went upstairs presumably to the room from where he had seen the orange being thrown.

In a few minutes the organ grinder returned to the lobby and left the building.

Clyde asked the desk clerk, "What was that all about?"

The clerk said, "He claimed somebody upstairs had killed his monkey."

A few days later the organ grinder was playing his music near the hotel minus the monkey. Clyde, feeling guilty, dropped a large bill in the organ grinders cup hoping the monkey could be replaced.

As they rounded the corner to their hotel, they passed a Mexican boy with a shoeshine kit. He followed them begging to shine their shoes.

Clyde said, "Let's get a shine."

"We've got on new shoes. They don't need a shine," replied Chester.

"Let's help the little feller out," Clyde insisted.

Chester said, "Just give him some money."

Clyde said, "Come on, let's get a shine." Clyde put his shoe on the boys' shine box and proceeded to get a shine.

Chester reluctantly let the Mexican boy shine his shoes.

When they got to their rooms upstairs, Chester looked down at his shoes and exclaimed to Clyde, "Look at your shoes!"

Their new black shoes had turned white. There is no telling what the boy had put on them. Chester kidded Clyde that the shine boy was probably the organ grinders son who was just getting even with them.

As the company had fidelity bond insurance covering employee fraud, Chester stayed in Mexico City to put together all the information needed to file a bond claim.

Information had been gathered substantiating the conversion of the company's inventory and product sales. Title to about $700,000 in company inventory converted by Jose was transferred back to company ownership.

Chester found that Jose had charged all the expenses of a daughter's wedding including dresses and the reception to the company. Many other goods and services for his personal benefit had also been charged to the company.

Chester engaged an interpreter who assisted in taking many statements from Mexican supplier company personnel to substantiate these charges and document the loss to the company.

Almost all the information then had been gathered on the fraud to attempt to obtain a final detailed statement from Jose.

In the meantime, two attorney's engaged by Jose approached Chester to negotiate a way to get their client out of jail.

Chester spent all day with the two attorneys and an interpreter discussing Jose's plight. Finally, by the end of the day the attorneys told Chester that they could convince their client to give a detailed signed statement if Chester would pay them $10,000.

The attorneys were informed that there was no way they would be paid for helping obtain a statement. After Jose spent more time in jail, he would be begging to give a statement.

Chester felt he needed further corroboration of ownership of the two companies that had been established by Jose for use in the fraud for support in the bond claim.

Chester was able to get the company's New York auditor back to Mexico City to assist in gathering information. They decided to go to the office Jose had maintained at

Mexican Jailbird

the top of a local ten-story building. Chester was hopeful of finding the corporate minute book, corporate stock register and other pertinent corporate records to prove Jose's ownership.

The auditor and Chester entered the office-building lobby and went to the elevator. They noted that the wiring was stripped out of the elevator panel for the button designating the tenth floor. This would not allow the elevator to go to that floor.

In addition, there was a government sign posting the 10th floor as off limits, meaning it was against the law to go to that floor. Apparently, Jose had not paid the local taxes when due for his personal corporations.

The auditor turned to Chester and said, "Well, I guess we are out of luck."

Chester told the auditor, "Let's go outside and see what we can do."

They noted that the building next door was just identical to the building they had just left. The buildings were spaced about 10 feet or more apart.

Chester told the auditor, "If we can get to the top of this building, we can jump across to the next building and gain access to Jose's office."

About that time a teen-age Mexican boy came down the sidewalk.

Chester asked him, "How would you like to make a hundred dollars?"

The Mexican boy looked at Chester like he was crazy. Chester finally raised the ante to three hundred dollars.

He told the Mexican boy that they needed his help in going to the top of this building and jumping across to the other building to get some of their records out of tenth floor office. They told the boy that they had lost the key and couldn't get into their office.

Chester figured if the Mexican boy could make the jump successfully to the other building so could he and the auditor.

All three went to the top of the building. Chester finally convinced the young man to jump from the ninth floor roof to the roof on top of the ninth floor building next door. The tenth floor offices were set back several feet from the ninth floor roof. The young man successfully made the jump and Chester chided the auditor to go next.

The auditor said they didn't pay him enough to do anything that crazy. Chester finally cajoled the auditor to jump. When the auditor also successfully made the jump, Chester figured he could make it as well.

They were able to raise a side window to gain entrance into the office. Chester told the auditor, "Gather up anything that looks like corporate or accounting records and then let's get out of here."

Just as they started through the file cabinets, they heard police cars with sirens blazing coming their way.

Chester found the corporate records he was looking for and told the auditor, "Grab whatever is handy and let's jump back across to the other building before the police get here."

They jumped across to the other building and rode the elevator down to the ground floor. Just then several police cars passed in front of the building and thankfully went on down the street.

Chester gladly paid the Mexican boy who walked off down the sidewalk shaking his head about the crazy gringo's.

Heading back to the hotel, the auditor told Chester, "You are crazy. I'm getting out of here before you cook up something else for me to do. I'm going back to New York now before anything else happens."

And he did.

The records obtained provided conclusive proof that Jose owned the two companies used in his fraud.

The stock certificate register showed Jose owned all the stock in the companies. The minute books disclosed that he was also the president of the companies as well as being the registered agent.

Chester then felt that enough information had been gathered to file a bond claim with the exception of obtaining a detailed statement from Jose admitting all aspects of his fraud.

Clyde brought a stunning blonde secretary to Mexico City with him to take a shorthand statement from Jose. Mexican men reportedly went bananas over good-looking blondes.

The three of them went to the jail to see Jose. He was brought out and put in a little barred three by five foot room.

He was very gaunt and a nervous wreck. Jose begged for a cigarette. He had a severe case of the shakes and looked very gaunt. He proclaimed sorrow for what he had done and asked for mercy, pleading to be released from jail.

After being told that the blonde was there to take down his statement, Jose asked, if he told us everything, would we get him out of jail? Clyde replied yes. He asked the blonde to go out with him that night after he got out of jail. He was obviously smitten with her.

Clyde had told the blonde that Jose was married and had at least five children but to agree with him if it would help get him to talk. They weren't going to let him out of jail anyway until they safely returned home.

They discussed in detail all their findings with the jailed man. Jose confirmed everything they had found. A statement was dictated to the secretary covering all aspects of the fraud. The secretary typed the statement and gave it to Jose to read. He agreed with all the facts in the statement.

A Mexican Federal Notary was summoned to witness Jose sign his statement of confession.

As they left the jail, the blonde waved goodbye and said she was looking forward to seeing Jose that night.

The three returned back to the states that night. Jose remained in jail for several more weeks before being released.

After recovery of the client's product inventories and other items, the remaining loss to the company was just over $385,000.

Chester filed a fidelity insurance bond claim on behalf of the company to recover the remaining $385,000.of loss. A few months later the claim was paid and the matter closed.

DON'T CROSS THE BORDER

A local bank requested that Clyde and Chester review a loan file covering a $2,000,000 loan made to a Mexican national customer.

The loan was over one year past due. Various attempts by the bank to collect the loan amount plus interest had been unsuccessful.

As this assignment appeared to be primarily a paperwork review, Chester agreed to handle the case.

At the bank, Chester began reviewing all the supporting documents behind the loan and the loan agreement. Although the Mexican national had several purported business interests in the United States, the loan proceeds were to be used for expansion of business interests in Mexico.

The signed personal financial statement provided the bank in conjunction with obtaining the loan set forth over $3,000,000 in assets in the United States with several million dollars in assets also located in Mexico.

For some unknown reason the bank had not verified the assets in the United States nor collateralized such assets against the loan.

When the bank loan became due, the Mexican national refused to make payment. His permanent residence address was located in central Mexico. All written communications to him in Mexico received no response.

Chester began the review by pursuing the assets shown as located in the United States. Most of the assets on the personal financial statements were real estate rental projects.

A review of the appropriate county courthouse records disclosed that the Mexican national had sold all the assets just prior to presenting the financial statement to the bank. Therefore, there were no assets that could potentially be attached in the United States. Pursuit of assets in Mexico appeared to hold little promise.

The files also disclosed that the Mexican national had no living relatives in the United States.

After completing a review of the files and information gained from the records, Chester believed that the only possibility of effecting collection of the loan might be to pursue a federal criminal action against the Mexican national for filing a false and fraudulent financial statement with the bank as an inducement to make the loan.

The bank was a national bank that could facilitate such action. Chester rationalized that if the Mexican National could be placed in jail in the United States he would figure out a way within a few weeks to pay off the loan balance.

Chester proposed this course of action with the bank officials. He acknowledged that this approach would only work if police on the United States side of the United States-Mexican border could pick up the Mexican National.

However, this possibility seemed unlikely, as the man had not been back across the border since shortly after making the loan.

The bank agreed to proceed with criminal charges. Chester agreed to pursue formulating a plan to try and get the man back into the United States in order that the police could pick him up.

Chester began interviewing all the people identified that had previously done business with the Mexican national in the United States.

After several interviews in various cities, Chester got lucky. He located a man who had just learned that the Mexican national's brother was in very bad health and had just been brought across the border into the United States and placed in a local hospital for treatment.

Going to the hospital, Chester was able to verify that the brother was in fact in the hospital and not expected to live much longer. Under those circumstances, Chester felt it likely that the Mexican national would try to quickly and quietly slip in and out of the country to visit his brother before he died.

Clyde made arrangements for a federal marshal to be available to pick up the Mexican national if and when he appeared at the hospital. The hospital room was placed under surveillance to identify the man if and when he arrived.

Sure enough, on the second day, the Mexican national arrived at the hospital room to see his brother. The federal marshal was called and told where the Mexican national could be located.

The marshal promptly went to the hospital where he arrested the surprised man and took him to jail.

After a couple of weeks in jail, the Mexican national asked for a meeting with the bank officials. He asked what he had to do to get out of jail.

He was told, "Pay off your debt!"

Within a week he had made arrangements for over $2,000,000 to be transferred to a U. S. bank in order that the bank could be paid in full.

After payment, arrangements were made for him to be released from jail and returned to Mexico.

Later he probably reminisced, "Oh, if I just hadn't crossed the border."

BEWARE THE CON MAN

When Chester first began his involvement in fraud investigations, Clyde gave him a book to read entitled "The Fountain Pen Conspiracy." The author of the book was a convicted felon currently in an eastern federal penitentiary. He had stolen and conned a lot of money during his criminal career. His book stated that if a person was going to launch a criminal career that banks and insurance companies were the easiest targets. He stated that too many junior employees were involved in the money end where they were easy to con. These employees were busy trying to make loans to prove their worth and advance in the company. Without proper experience they were susceptible to make bad deals. Also when loans were brought to the loan committee, many deals were made that if you vote for my loan I will vote for yours. Therefore the substance of the loans was never properly reviewed.

Adding credence to the opinions stressed in the book, a local bank, through various agents, owned a 100 percent interest in a financiera (a savings and loan institution in Mexico).

For business reasons, sale of the financiera became desirable.

A group of individuals previously unknown to the financiera management in Mexico offered to purchase 51 percent of the outstanding common stock in the financiera for $1,200,000 U.S.

No preliminary in-depth investigation was made by the bank as to the responsibility and reliability of the purchasing group except to determine that the lead man was a French national and the other three were presumably wealthy Mexican businessmen.

The purchase offer was accepted. The bank's cost in the remaining 49 percent interest in the common stock in the financiera was $736,000 U.S.

One of the conditions of sale sought and obtained by the purchasing group was that the board of directors would be nine in number with five to be appointed by the new group. The French national became chairman of the board.

The new chairman was given broad and almost complete authority to run the affairs of the financiera and to alone grant loans up to 700,000 pesos ($56,000 U.S.) and to make loans from 700,000 pesos to 1,000,000 pesos ($80,000 U.S.) with the signature of the chairman and one of the other three of his directors. All loans over 1,000,000 pesos required the signature by a board member representative of the 49 percent stock ownership interest.

Immediately after the consummation of the sale, the former commissario (outside independent auditor) was asked to resign and was replaced by a firm chosen by the new chairman of the board.

In the days following closing of the sale, the business of the financiera seemed to expand rapidly with securing a great number of certificates of deposits and making a great number of loans.

About six months later the financiera collapsed. The Mexican Banking Commission assumed control over the assets and business operations.

The local bank's investment of $736,000 U.S. in 49 percent of their remaining common stock became worthless.

The Mexican Banking Commission advised that they were going to pursue criminal charges against the local bank's Mexican representatives.

The local bank requested that Clyde and Chester assist the Mexican Banking Commission in investigating the cause of the collapse of the financiera and determine if any monetary recoveries could be made.

Based on their investigation, the following series of events were uncovered.

Investigation disclosed that the purchasing group had made a 30-day loan of 15,000,000 pesos ($1,200,000 U.S.) from another Mexican financiera just prior to purchase of the 51 percent stock interest.

After assuming control of the financiera, monies were taken out of the financiera via fictitious loans to repay the original loan. In effect, the purchasing group acquired control of the financiera with the financiera's own money.

Also, immediately after the sale, the purchasing group formed seven "straw" corporations that were capitalized for only nominal amounts.

The purchasing group proceeded to grant loans to these corporations for sums just less than 1,000,000 pesos limit and make loans to themselves individually in varying amounts up to 700,000 pesos.

These "straw" corporations were the front for purchase of seven tracts of commercial land in various parts of Mexico. The purchase price paid for such tracts was in every instance several times the appraised value of the land.

The land purchased was indirectly owned by the insiders who used the above devise to divert funds to their own use from the financiera.

The minutes of the board of directors meetings had been retyped to insert loans of this type after the minutes had been signed and approved by the bank's representatives of the 49 percent ownership interest.

Over a period of six months after the purchase, the purchasing group had made improper loans from the financiera of about 105,000,000 pesos ($8,040,000 U.S.) representing substantially all of the firm's capital and customers' deposits.

When it was evident that the banking commission together with Clyde and Chester were discovering the improprieties, most of the purchasing group disappeared.

It was later learned that one of the well-to-do Mexicans in the 51% ownership interest group had also been swindled out of $2,000,000 U.S. through purchase from the Frenchman of fraudulent certificates of deposit drawn on a Miami bank.

About $4,000,000 U.S. of the amount obtained through improper loans was transferred out of Mexico to the United States where it was used to make down payments on the purchase of controlling interests in Dallas and Miami banks.

Ownership in these banks was lost when the balance of the purchase price could not be paid, as there were no more funds for the purchasing group to take from the financiera.

The Mexican banking authorities sought to bring criminal charges against the group. However, the French national fled to Spain and the Mexicans to the United States. The Mexican government took over control of the financiera and made good the customers' deposits.

Unfortunately, the local bank had no choice but to write off the balance of its $736,000 U.S. investment in the financiera as there was no means of recovery.

However, based on the findings of Clyde and Chester's investigation, the Mexican Banking Commission agreed to drop criminal charges against the local bank's Mexican representatives. They had not benefited financially from the fraud. They had just been royally duped and conned.

STORE SITE ACQUISITIONS

A client had made many land acquisitions in Canada for the purpose of building an auto parts centers. Since only one employee had located the sites and negotiated the purchase of each land acquisition, the client asked that all purchase agreements be reviewed to determine if possible fraud had occurred. Although the employee was not under suspicion, the client wanted to determine that there had not occurred any kickbacks to the employee by the sellers. Purchases from some of the same sellers were to be reviewed. Comp prices for similar land sales near the acquired locations were also to be reviewed.

Chester went to the central office in Canada and gathered over 200 land acquisition files. Over the next few weeks Chester reviewed the land purchases in all the areas stressed by the company to determine that the terms and price of each acquisition was proper and according to company policy.

Chester made a physical observation of many of the land sites to determine that all locations complied with company criteria including zoning and other related restrictions. Comps near the land locations were independently verified. No multiple purchases from the same seller were found. A search was made to determine the validity of each seller. No restrictions existed on construction at any of the land sites.

After an exhaustive review of each acquisition, no improprieties were uncovered.

Chester discussed his review with Clyde. Clyde and Chester agreed that no further review would be productive and polygraphing the employee was not necessary.

A report of the review was submitted to appropriate management and the assignment concluded.

ACCUSING THE ACCUSER

When a Canadian business owner set up a branch operation in Houston, he was fortunate to obtain a substantial amount of business from a large well-known local business. After four years of operations, about 80% of the branch office revenue originated from this one source.

When the largest customer accused the local branch office of giving kickbacks to their employees and canceled all its business contracts with the branch office, the Canadian owner hired a local law firm to represent his business.

The former customer had told the Canadian that criminal proceedings were going to be pursued against his local branch office and its employees.

As the accusations covered charges that might either be substantiated or refuted from the client's books and records, the law firm requested Chester to assist in investigating the charges.

At a meeting with six of the law firm representatives and the client, the client set forth the accusations.

The former largest branch customer had accused the Canadian client of providing excessive gratuities and cash payments to its employees in order to obtain business. If the charges were shown to be true, the client would have to close his business due to the loss of 80% of its revenue from this one major customer.

The client said he had not authorized nor approved any payments or gratuities to the customer's employees. He had been flabbergasted when this accusation was made. When he questioned the branch employees, they denied the accusations.

The client advised that he had gone through the local branch office records and no such payments could be found. As some of the payments and business was handled out of Canada, it was possible that payments might have originated from one of the Canadian offices without his knowledge or approval.

The lawyers suggested that Chester make a complete audit of the client's local books to determine if any gratuities had been provided. After completion of that review, the lawyers suggested that Chester then spend several days performing audits at the two Canadian offices which were at opposite ends of Canada.

Although the fee income was enticing from such a review, Chester felt like the client was going to occur substantial expense with an undo loss of time before any possible result could be obtained. By the time the audits were finished, the client's branch office would be closed and all business lost.

Accusing The Accuser

In sizing up the client, Chester believed him to be an honorable man. Chester's dealings in Canada with Canadian businessmen in the past had proven them to operate at a high level of integrity.

After the lawyers finished their presentation, the client turned to Chester and asked him what he would recommend.

Chester replied that the lawyers might not like what he was going to say. Chester said, "You have very little time to right this matter or your business here is gone."

Chester advised that he had previously dealt with his major customer and in those cases he found that it was the customer's employees who were putting the arm on suppliers for gratuities.

He advised they could either go the long route as suggested by the attorneys or take a short cut.

Chester proposed taking a short cut in which they would leave that afternoon for Canada. Chester would review the books and interview the client's supervisory employees. If everything went according to plan and no "gratuity" payments were found, Chester felt they would be on their way home by the next night and ready to confront the customer to refute the allegations. Chester said he couldn't guarantee that the short cut approach would work.

The attorneys asked the client what he wanted to do.

The client turned to Chester and said, "I like your idea and I'm going to stake my business on you."

This was a large order and one that did not make the attorneys happy as they had looked forward to this case producing substantial billing hours.

One of the attorneys, the client and Chester left for Canada that afternoon. Chester had requested that the client have his supervisory personnel in the office for him to interview that night. In addition, Chester requested that personnel in the other Canadian office be available by conference call to discuss the matter that night by telephone.

On arrival in Canada, they proceeded to the client's office. Chester began interviewing the supervisory employees and reviewing the books. After completing the review, Chester had pieced together the following story.

The client had purchased a 27-foot fishing boat and docked it near the Gulf of Mexico for employee fishing trips.

On one occasion, the branch office employee had taken employees of the former largest customer out on the boat on a fishing trip. Several days later, one of those customer employees telephoned and requested that he be allowed to borrow the boat to go fishing.

The Canadian client's branch employees were afraid to refuse and loaned him the boat.

When the boat had not been returned in a few days, the customer's employee was telephoned with a request to return the boat. The man replied that he didn't plan to return the boat at that time.

As time passed, the customer's employee was telephoned several times about the boat. In each instance he replied that he was not ready to return the boat.

The Canadian branch office had heard rumors that the customer's employee had transferred title to the boat into his own name. The client's employees had not told their boss of this event, as they were afraid of repercussions.

Further discussion revealed that several of the customer's employees had put the arm on the client's employees for substantial gratuities that in most cases had not been granted.

Statements were taken from the client's Canadian employees setting forth what had been learned. In addition, Chester obtained canceled checks covering minor payments for goods that had been provided the customer's employees.

Much to Chester's joy, through further interviews with other client employees in Canada, he discovered that one employee had obtained a copy of the original title to the boat in question and later a copy of the title registered in the name of the customer employee.

The Canadian employee had been able to obtain a copy of the new title from the appropriate state records office. As their boss had been in the U.S. for several weeks, he had not communicated these findings to him.

Upon initiating a conference telephone call with the other Canadian office employees Chester learned nothing new. All payments and business related to the customer had been handled out of the office that Chester had just conducted his review.

At midnight Chester filled in the client with his findings and said, "Let's go home. I have what I need to resolve the problem."

The client marveled at what Chester had discovered in that short period of time and asked what would happen next.

Accusing The Accuser

Chester advised that as soon as they got home he would request a meeting with the customer's general counsel and security manager. Chester felt they could resolve the matter quickly.

As Chester suggested, a meeting was held in Chester's office the next day. The two men from the customer's office arrived and immediately said they weren't going to waste time. They were going down to the district attorney's office now and file charges against Chester's client.

Chester replied, "Fine, can I ride down there with you?"

The general counsel and security manager said, "What do you mean, you want to go with us!"

Chester replied, "I think you will find the meeting interesting. It will be your employee going to jail instead of ours. In addition, we plan to sue you for improperly canceling our work contracts."

The two men said, "Wait a minute, what are you talking about?"

Chester showed them copies of the client employee's statements, canceled checks, and the two titles to the boat.

The general counsel turned to Chester and asked, "What do you want? I think we can make a deal."

Chester advised that the client wanted his boat back. If the business contracts were reinstated, then criminal proceedings would not be pursued at that time.

However, if the client's business with their firm was further jeopardized by the customer's employees, criminal actions would be initiated and the newspaper flooded with bad publicity.

The general counsel agreed to these terms and it was business as usual with the client before the end of the day. The boat was returned the next day.

Once again Chester had gotten lucky. The client was very happy with the conclusion.

However, Chester never got any more business from that law firm. They weren't very happy with such a short case and so few billable hours.

THE ONE THAT GOT AWAY

Clyde and Chester were asked to investigate cash shortages at several gas stations and convenience stores in South Florida. They were furnished a company jet airplane for their use.

Upon their arrival, they reviewed cash procedures in the stores that had experienced cash shortages. They found that over a three-day period, cash deposits to the bank were about $75,000 short. Bank deposits from each store were to be picked up by a regional assistant manager each evening and placed in the night depository at a local bank.

When Clyde and Chester sought out the regional assistant manager, he could not be found.

When inquiries were made at his apartment, the apartment manager said the man we sought had suddenly moved out the night before. In further questioning, he stated that his former tenant had relatives in Kingston, Jamaica.

As the former assistant manager had probably fled to Jamaica with the company's money, they decided to take the airplane to Kingston in an attempt to locate him.

What they didn't realize that in order to get to Jamaica they would have to fly directly over Cuba.

The airplane pilots forgot to file a flight plan requesting permission to fly over Cuba. As they approached Cuba, five Cuban MIG fighter airplanes suddenly surrounded their airplane.

They were shocked and the pilots panicked. They could hear the Cuban fighter pilots speaking to them via the radio on their airplane. Since the Cuban's were speaking in Spanish no one knew what was being said.

All the pilots could do was fly straight ahead and hope for the best. The fighter airplanes followed them until they had crossed over Cuba and then the MIG's turned back. They sighed in obvious relief. The jet they were in was no match for the MIGs.

Landing in Kingston, they checked into a local hotel and began searching for the relatives of the former Miami employee.

The director of security at the hotel was a former local policeman. With his assistance, an address was obtained for a person thought to be a relative of the former employee.

The One That Got Away

Clyde and Chester went outside the hotel to hail a taxi to take them to the street address. They hoped to con the former employee into flying back to Miami where they would have him arrested.

It was almost dark as they approached a taxi driver. Chester gave the address to the driver and told him he would pay him $100 if he would take them to that address and wait for them to return. One Hundred Dollars in Kingston then was equal to about an average month's pay.

The taxi driver turned to Chester and said, "No Mon."

Chester then said he would give him $200 and received the same reply. Chester finally raised the number to $500. The taxi driver again shook his head no.

Chester asked him, "What is the problem?"

The driver replied, "Mon that a bad part of town. They smokes that bad weed and those dudes are higher than a kite. They bad. They carry big pistols. I drives you there and they see your white faces shining in the moonlight they fires into the car and blows out the tires. They rolls the car over on its side. Then they pours gasoline on the car, sets it on fire, and shoots us when we crawl out. No way Mon I take you there."

They went into the hotel and studied a map of the city. They found a way to get around the reportedly bad area in the city to within a few blocks of where they thought their man might be hiding. They didn't believe the area could be as bad as the taxi driver had represented.

They finally convinced another taxi driver to go around the area in question and let them out a few blocks from the address. The cab driver agreed to wait for them there.

Chester and Clyde, dressed in dark clothes, eased down the street until they found a house at the address they had obtained. A light was on inside. They knocked on the door. No one came to the door. They continued to knock.

Suddenly Chester felt a knife at his back.

A voice whispered, "What you want Mon?"

Chester replied that they wanted to talk to his U. S. relative currently visiting him at that address.

The voice whispered back that he never heard of such a person. He said, "Mon you not out of here now, you won't be able to leave."

They beat a hasty trail out of there back to the taxi.

Investigating Corporate Fraud

Arriving back at the hotel, they told the hotel director of security about their experience. He said he wasn't surprised, as a lot of people had been killed in that area.

Chester asked the security man if he worked any security matters during his off time.

He advised that he did.

Clyde told him we would give him $5,000 if he would pick up our man and put him on an airplane to Miami. A local policeman would be requested to pick him up at the airport and book him into jail.

The security man said he would be able to do that within three days.

Clyde asked him to call collect every-day and advise of his progress on the matter.

They returned home. Not having heard anything from the security man in four days, Chester called the hotel in Kingston and asked to speak to the director of security.

Chester was told that he was no longer there. Chester asked, "What do you mean he is no longer there?"

Chester was told that the security man was dead. He had been killed across town on an off duty job the night before.

To this day, they don't know if the man was killed trying to bring their man back. They just knew they weren't going back to Jamaica looking for him.

THE MEXICAN SCARE

In a review of a produce import operation at a Texas border town, Chester found that the company had advanced over $ 1,000,000 to Mexican growers against produce they would ship to the company in season. These advances were made in direct violation of company policy. When the season opened, the company discovered that the Mexican growers had sold their produce to other customers thus pocketing the money the company had advanced. The Mexican growers could not be located.

Since these advances were not authorized and resulted in substantial loss to the company, the office was closed and all employees terminated.

Later Chester and Clyde were informed that the Mexican growers who pocketed the advances were now headquartered in Guadalajara, Mexico. Clyde and Chester took a company airplane to Guadalajara in an attempt to recover the loss. The fog was so thick when approaching Guadalajara that landing was impossible. The airplane was diverted to Puerto Vallarta. After waiting for a couple of hours, the fog cleared and they were cleared to fly to Guadalajara.

When boarding the airplane, the airport police refused to let the airplane depart until they were paid $ 10,000. This obviously was a holdup without a gun. The pilots refused to make payment. Clyde and Chester were told to go into town for a few hours while they resolved this matter. After eating and shopping down town, they returned to the airport. In the meantime the pilots had negotiated the holdup fee down to $ 500 that was reluctantly paid. Then they were on their way to Guadalajara.

After making several inquires about the Mexican growers whereabouts in Guadalajara, we learned that their headquarters had moved to the Culiacan and Los Mochis area. Preparing to fly to Culiacan they were told that area was the center of one of the most vicious Drug Lords in Mexico. They were told that it could be fatal to go there. They were also told that the airplane would be seized and never be recovered. The pilots advised that based on that information, they would not take the airplane to Culiacan.

Having hit a dead-end, they had no choice but to return home empty handed with no recoveries.

BERMUDA CASH FLOW

Chester was asked to review records in the company's Bermuda insurance office. When the company planned to self-insure, a corporation was organized in Bermuda to receive both domestic and foreign funds equivalent to the insurance premiums that would have been charged by the various insurance companies. In effect the company was insuring itself against property and other losses.

Millions of dollars were transferred to the Bermuda office from the mainland and overseas operations. Funds received from the United States were moved into investments in the United States. Obviously, this arrangement was made to avoid Federal Income Taxes on earnings in the United States that was perfectly proper under the U.S. Tax Code.

Funds received from foreign companies were in turn invested primarily in Europe.

The Bermuda office contained the investment documents, stocks and bond certificates, etc. in a vault at a local bank. Chester verified all the proper investment documents were present and properly reflected on the company's books.

Chester's review also centered on examining and verifying cash receipts and transfers to the appropriate locations. Funds that were used to make investments in the United States were routed through several banks that ultimately ended up in a designated New York bank.

All investment documents were in order. However, monies transferred to the designated bank in New York were being routed first to a Canadian bank, then to several other banks in Canada and the states before arriving 11 days later to the New York bank. This meant that each bank along the way received investment income for the time funds were held thus depriving the company use of the funds for 11 days.

The manager of the insurance company had been in the office for two years and was just following the system he inherited. No fraud appeared involved. Whoever set up that system from the home office had established the funds routing for no apparent reason. It is possible that the routing had been initially dictated by the New York bank to flow cash through their correspondent banks. Chester made arrangements for all transfer of funds to be made directly to the applicable New York bank. This saved the company considerable time and money and gave the company access to same day funds.

BEWARE THE CANADIAN JAILHOUSE

Clyde and Chester were requested to conduct an investigation at a Canadian automotive parts manufacturing plant. The plant had experienced sudden losses over the past few months.

The accounting/office was small with only a secretary, inventory and stock clerk, two accounting clerks, and controller.

A review of the parts receiving, storage, and inventory procedures indicated no shortages.

A review of the cash disbursements indicated payments to certain new office supply and maintenance companies had received no business in the past. An investigation into these companies involved found that such companies did not exist.

Cash disbursements showed that the controller had sole invoice approval. The payment checks were drawn and paid by the office secretary. This event led Chester to believe that the controller had set up fictitious companies used to convert cash to his personnel gain.

Clyde interviewed the controller after the other employees had left for the day, confronting him with the evidence found. After a period of denials, the controller finally admitted his theft. He had issued and approved invoices from his fictitious companies for maintenance and services not performed. He then had checks paid to his fictitious companies. When checks issued during the day were given to the controller for mailing, he pulled out those envelopes with the checks payable to his companies and placed the proceeds into his personal bank account. Over the past 3 months he had stolen $ 46,500. He had used the money to try and impress a new girl friend with jewelry and clothes.

A call to the local police station brought out a police investigator who reviewed the statement Clyde had obtained. He then took his own statement covering the same detail. Before he took the controller to jail, the policeman asked Clyde and Chester if they would like to stay until the trail. In the United States it would normally take 6 months or more before a case like this would come to trial. (This event took place on a Friday afternoon.) The policeman was advised that they could not stay all the time it would take for the case to come to trial. The policeman stated it might take a long time in your country before a case comes to trial. But here the controller will be tried on Monday and he will be headed to the pen by Monday afternoon.

No recoveries of money could be made from the controller. The company's fidelity insurance bond deductible was over the amount of the loss so no recovery of the loss could be made. Justice is swift in Canada.

SHIPBUILDING

PAINT AND LEAD CAPER

Clyde and Chester were requested to go to a shipbuilding and repair facility that had recently been acquired by the company. The company suspected considerable fraud might be taking place. The executive stated that there were only three reasons a company like this one was on the market; 1) They could not raise money for operations or expansion; 2) Management was old and tired, out of touch with the times; or 3) There was massive fraud. In most cases he thought it was all three.

There were over 30,000 employees working at the plant location. While walking around inside the plant grounds trying to decide where to start the review, they noted two employees driving a Cushman motor scooter toward the fence line with what appeared to be two 10-gallon cans and a block of some kind of material.

They observed the men bending the bottom of the fence back towards the parking lot where employees parked their cars. The men then pushed the cans and what appeared to be lead under the fence beside one of the cars.

Since it was only about an hour before the plant shift change, they waited inside the plant near the fence line to see what happened next.

Shortly, the same two men walked down the plant employee parking lot to the fence area previously observed and loaded the two 10 gallon cans and lead into the back of their car. The license number of the car was noted.

In determining what was in the cans, they learned the plant had a facility that produced paint that was placed into ten-gallon cans. The only color produced was gray.

They also learned that large amounts of lead were being used in other plant operations. The lead was purchased in 60-pound pigs each. The lead was primarily being used as ship ballast.

After obtaining information on the registered owner of the car, they drove that evening to the area where the identified employees lived. To their amazement, almost every house in about a ten-square block area was painted shipyard gray.

The next morning, the identified employees were called into the office and Clyde began interviewing them. Signed statements were obtained wherein the employees confessed that they had stolen about four ten gallon cans of paint and two pigs of lead each week over a 24 year period.

They stated that a paint contracting company owned by them was used to paint houses in the area with the stolen paint. The lead was sold to fishermen along the waterfront for use in making lead sinkers and fishing boat ballast.

Paint And Lead Caper

Chester calculated that the thefts had cost the client over $124,000 during the previous 24 years.

A fidelity insurance bond covered all plant employees. Chester filed an insurance claim to recover the loss.

The two employees were turned over to the authorities for prosecution.

This was only the first of many frauds being perpetrated at this location that were discovered over the next several months. Several of these frauds will be covered in subsequent chapters.

OVER THE FENCE THEY WILL GO

While at the same location as the "Paint and Lead Caper" fraud covered in the prior chapter, Clyde and Chester were sitting in their rental car at 7:00 am one morning observing 30,000 employees file through the entrance gate to clock in for work.

A few minutes after seven they noted that several employees were jumping over the fence at the north side of the plant premises. They counted about 80 employees jumping the fence.

They could only conclude that the employees had entered the plant, clocked in, and were heading up the street to who knows where. Leaving the car they followed the employees for about six blocks.

The employees entered a beat-up-looking-building that was owned by a ship's repair competitor of the company.

Previously at the plant, they had learned that the company had lost several major repair jobs to the competitor. The company could not understand how it was being under-bid on the jobs or how the competitor had enough skilled employees to perform an acceptable job.

They took turns during the day observing the competitors operation. About 10 minutes before 4:00 pm, they noted the company's employees were leaving the competitors plant. They headed down the street to their permanent place of employment. The employees jumped back over the fence into the plant, presumably clocked out, and left the plant.

Thus it appeared that the employees were paid a days work by the company and then went down the street to the competitors plant, worked all day, and earned an additional day's pay.

From an unnamed source, they were able to obtain a copy of the competitor's employee payroll list. The names on the list were compared to the company's employee payroll list. Sure enough, about 95 names were found on the lists. However, the competitor was paying only about 70% of the hourly rate paid by the client.

The next day Clyde began interviewing the 95 identified employees and after taking signed statements covering their improper activities, the employees were terminated.

While Clyde was finishing with the "fence jumpers", Chester began reviewing surplus material and scrap sales.

Chester selected one major job he had heard was finished the year before that reportedly had about $10,000,000 of new surplus stainless steel products left over from that project.

Checks of inventory files and records together with interviews of several appropriate personnel failed to disclose any information relative to the surplus parts. No one seemed to know, or would admit, knowing anything about the surplus. No inventory records could be found. No sale of these parts could be found.

As the type of materials left over on that job appeared to be the same type that could be used by the local ship's repair competitor, Chester felt there was a possibility that the competitor was somehow getting the company's new surplus materials at bargain prices.

If the competitor were getting labor at 70% of the company's cost and materials at a bargain price, this would explain why the company had lost bids on several major ship repair jobs.

Since the plant operation generated a lot of scrap material as well as surplus parts, the whole scrap and salvage operation became suspect.

Chester reviewed the available records to determine which companies were the major buyers of surplus and salvage. It was not until later they learned that most of the scrap yards on the East Coast were reportedly controlled by the mob.

Chester and Clyde started interviewing scrap dealers in the area to find out how they obtained the company's business.

In their first visit to a local small scrap operation owned by a man who was reportedly honest, they introduced themselves and stated their business.

The owner, who was about seventy years old, started bragging about how young he felt. He said he could kick out the light bulb hanging high over his head. To demonstrate, he stepped back and proceeded to kick the light bulb.

Clyde exclaimed, "Wow, you sure are agile."

The owner grabbed Clyde by the throat and said, "Don't you cuss me man."

Chester had to pull him off shouting, "No! No! He's not cursing you, agile means you are quick, nimble and active."

The owner grumbled, "Well, OK then."

Clyde was able to cultivate his trust and received much helpful background information on many scrap dealers in the area.

About 9:00 pm the next night, they were driving around the area surveying various scrap dealer operations when they noticed a light on in a scrap dealer's office. They decided to go in and talk with whoever was inside.

Upon entering the office, a man looked up from his desk and said, "Well, Clyde and Chester. I wondered when you would stop by."

They looked at each other in amazement, as they had no idea that anyone there would know their names.

The man reached into a desk drawer and tossed a big brown envelope onto the desk. He paused about a minute, and then reached into another desk drawer and pulled out a 45-caliber pistol, pointing it at them.

He said, "There is $50,000 cash in the envelope." Then shaking the pistol at them, he said, "Take your pick, which one do you want?"

They looked at each other in amazement. They turned and walked toward the door, with Chester stating, "If you shoot us, you'll have to shoot us in the back."

Driving off in their rental car, they knew they were getting close to a big-time scrap fraud as somebody was beginning to feel the heat.

They then decided it was time to investigate the entire surplus and salvage operation. Most of the client's plant scrap generated was being shipped out by rail car. The rail cars were pulled onto the company's weight scale, weighed, and moved out of the plant.

They reviewed the weight scale procedures.

They noted that inside the scale room, weight tickets were stacked to the ceiling all around the room. They were told that copies of the tickets were kept for years and years in case any question came up about the weight of any rail car. This seemed ridiculous.

Clyde examined the scales and noticed that by just moving the scale apparatus with his finger he could print out any weight from zero to 200,000 pounds. Suspecting that the weight man had some kind of deal going, Clyde took him aside and began interrogating him.

In a little while, the employee admitted that for over twenty-three years he had been shorting the weight on every rail car by a thousand pounds or more. For his endeavors, a local scrap dealer left a fifth of whiskey by the employee's car every Friday afternoon. The man's fraud had cost the company thousands and thousands of dollars over the years.

Since the local scrap dealers were taking advantage of the company's scrap and salvage sales, they then concluded that the scrap dealers were also fraudulently obtaining surplus materials and parts from the client. As the client's local plant competitor was using the clients labor, they then surmised that the competitor was also receiving materials and parts from the client.

Chester thought it probable that the local competitor had inside information on the client's surplus material availability. The competitor might be obtaining needed surplus parts from the company for their repair jobs.

Conducting a review of property records at the courthouse, Chester learned the competitor company owned an old building at the edge of town.

Driving by the location late at night, they noted bars on all the windows. The building appeared to be well secured although there were no guards in the area. Looking through the windows, they observed that the building appeared to be used to store materials and parts. Chester speculated that some of the company's surplus materials might be inside.

With the assistance from a local police investigator, they were able to enter the building. They found that the building was substantially full of surplus materials and parts obviously all obtained from the company.

Chester also found the inventory records covering $10,000,000 in surplus parts left over from a ship construction that he had previously been searching for at the plant. The company's name was still on each inventory card. It appeared that the competitor had obtained all the new surplus $10,000,000 in parts together with the applicable inventory records.

Suspecting that the company's scrap and salvage manager had a hand in this matter, they returned to the client's office where Clyde began interrogating him concerning their suspicions.

After an hour or so of denials, the manager finally admitted to having sold the $10,000,000 in new surplus parts to a scrap dealer for $70,000. He knew that the parts were destined for the client's competitor. The manager admitted to receiving a used Pontiac worth about $3,000 for making the deal.

As the whole purchasing, scrap and salvage operation was so rotten and mired in fraud; they were able to obtain a Grand Jury investigation into all related matters at the company's plant.

The yearlong Grand Jury review resulted in several indictments and convictions of company employees and local involved persons.

Insurance bond claims were filed to recover the estimated company's loss.

THE BEACH HOUSE

During the Grand Jury investigation covered in the prior chapter, Clyde and Chester heard rumors that the maintenance superintendent had a very nice beach house on the North Carolina coast.

The rumors centered on the maintenance superintendent having received a beach house for favoritism given an east coast contractor on major maintenance projects at the plant.

They drove to North Carolina and checked property records in several counties. Title to a beachfront lot was found to be in the name of the maintenance superintendent's wife.

Based on the property description, they drove to the site on the beach. There they found a very nice beach house on the beachfront lot.

When they arrived back at the plant, Chester scheduled the amount of dollars spent with the contractor in question during the past five years.

Clyde then called the maintenance superintendent into the office. Clyde confronted him with the rumors and suspicions.

At first the superintendent denied any involvement but when confronted with being included in an ongoing Grand Jury investigation he broke down and confessed. He admitted that he had picked out the lot on the beach. He said that the contractor then paid for the lot.

Later on, the superintendent had plans drawn for a beach house and approached the contractor to pay for the construction costs. The contractor agreed to pay the cost of construction. The total out of pocket cost of the lot and house to the contractor approached $90,000 as the contractor's construction crews performed most of the work.

In exchange for the lot and house, the Superintendent approved fictitious change orders on the contractor's plant construction projects for work not performed.

The contract overcharges amounted to more than $500,000 during the prior five years.

As title to the beach house was in the name of the superintendent's wife, gaining title to the property as restitution was not probable without pursuing the matter through the courts.

After the former maintenance superintendent was prosecuted, they decided to pursue the contractor in an attempt to obtain recovery of the contractor's overcharges.

During a meeting with the contractor, they sought recovery of the $500,000 loss. As much of the work performed by the contractor indirectly involved work on government projects, it might be possible to use this lever against the contractor.

They told the contractor that if the plant wasn't reimbursed, the matter would be pursued with the appropriate governmental agency through the courts.

The contractor thought their threats were a bluff and refused to discuss making any restitution.

Chester met with the contractor on another occasion to no avail. When the last meeting terminated, Chester advised that the company's lawyer was reviewing the matter. He anticipated federal lawsuits to be filed and the government brought into the picture.

Chester pursued the matter with the company's attorneys. Two attorneys reviewing the matter scheduled a trip to Washington, D. C. One of the attorneys was scheduled to be sworn-in before the United States Supreme Court in order to be able to practice before that court.

As the contractor's office was near Washington, D. C., Chester scheduled a meeting with the contractor for late that same morning.

After they appeared before the Supreme Court, they went to the office of the Attorney General of the United States. One of the lawyers with Chester had been a former U. S. Attorney and knew several people in that office.

Since they were running late in getting to the contractor's office, Chester suddenly got an idea.

Chester asked a secretary in the attorney general's office if she would place a call to the president of the contracting firm. He asked her to announce that Chester was calling from the attorney general's office.

When the telephone call was placed and the secretary announced from where Chester was calling, near panic could be heard in the president's voice as he asked Chester, "What are you doing in Washington, D. C.?"

He advised that he had stopped by Washington, D. C. that morning to get all his ducks lined up concerning their mutual problem. Now that he had completed his inquiries, Chester wanted to meet that afternoon at 2:00 p.m. The president of the contracting firm agreed.

With the use of one of the company's airplanes, they flew to the city that the contractor's office was located.

Chester, with the attorneys, entered the office of the contractor's president. The contractor's general counsel and treasurer were also present.

Chester advised the president that he didn't want to waste time. Either he left now with a check for $500,000 or the matters reviewed in Washington, D. C. that morning would be pursued.

The bluff worked and the president instructed the treasurer to immediately go cut a check.

The general counsel and treasurer both voiced their disapproval of the company making any settlement.

The president turned to the treasurer and said, "I told you to go cut a check!"

In the meantime, the president asked if his company could obtain any future business from the company's plant.

Chester advised that he would be allowed to bid on all future projects along with other contractors. If he won the bids, he could expect that Chester would have all of his contract invoices and work audited in detail in the future.

When the treasurer arrived with the check, Chester suggested that they all go on the company's airplane to the plant located in another state. He advised the president that it would be a good idea for him to personally present the check to the president of the company.

Chester then said he would set forth their agreement covering future business.

The president agreed and told his general counsel and treasurer to come along. Neither liked to fly and did not want to go. Again the president ordered them to go and reluctantly, they agreed.

The check was delivered to the president of the company. The company had recovered the $ 500,000 loss. Future contract bidding arrangements were confirmed.

As the contractor obviously knew that he had potential problems if the government could be brought into the matter, the bluff Chester used had been successful.

THE TRAVELING LUGGAGE

While on the East Coast making a security review, Clyde and Chester became aware that a company ship's trial cruise was about to take place.

When the company completed construction of a large ship, the vessel was taken out to sea for a shake down cruise. Many local politicians and prominent citizens were invited to join the five-day sea trial cruise.

They heard rumors that in past years when ships returned from the shake down cruise everything not tied down disappeared from the ship.

Silverware, ashtrays, towels, dinnerware, and anything else that contained the insignia of the ship disappeared. This proved costly to the company.

However, due to the prominence of the individuals on such cruises, nothing had ever been done about this in the past. They decided to change this situation.

On the day that the sea trial was to begin, they observed the invited guests strolling through the plant gates with four suitcases under their arms. It was obvious by their walk that most of the suitcases were empty.

When the shake down cruise was over five days later, they were ready for them. A long table was set up just outside the employee entrance gate. Two policemen had been recruited from the city to inspect the suitcases of the departing guests.

A long line of guests formed at the exit gate. When the first of the returning guests came out the exit their luggage was inspected and found to contain silverware, towels, wash cloths, ash trays and everything else imaginable from the ship all bearing the ships insignia.

The first twenty guests were taken downtown, booked, and released.

The others in line quickly abandoned their luggage inside the plant grounds and walked out the plant empty handed. After all had departed, suitcase after suitcase full of souvenirs was found stashed beside the plant buildings and bushes.

These items were then returned to the ship.

Word of this surprise inspection circulated fast throughout the area. There were no more problems on future ship shake down cruises.

THE DIRTY DEAL

During a later review at the shipyard, Clyde and Chester were driving by the plant with the local plant security officer. They passed an area along the river where many dump trucks were backed up waiting to unload dirt for filling in a section of the river for an additional dry-dock.

Chester motioned for Clyde to stop the car. Chester asked the security officer how much dirt was being brought in.

He replied that he had heard in excess of a half million cubic yards.

Chester asked when had the trucks started bringing dirt to the plant.

He was told that this was about the end of the second or third week of deliveries.

Chester told them that he'd bet a hundred dollars that the plant was getting short deliveries and/or overcharged on the dirt as truckers are the best in the world at being able to short cut, bypass, or avoid prescribed internal control procedures.

Clyde told Chester, "Why don't you go down and check it out."

Chester went down to the guard gate receiving area and climbed up onto the trucks to observe the amount of dirt in order to verify that the trucks were fully loaded. He then observed the trucks being weighed inside the plant.

Chester then went down to the construction office to determine how the delivery tickets and weight slips were being handled. All copies of the weight slips were being forwarded to the contractor's office. No plant personnel observed the deliveries of dirt nor approved any of the paper work in the construction office. In other words there was no internal control over the dirt deliveries.

Later, copies of the weight slips were attached to the trucking company invoice sent to the plant for dirt delivered by each truck.

As previously stated no plant personnel were involved in viewing the dirt receiving procedure. Copies of the weight tickets were not signed as receipts or kept by company plant personnel to be later matched with the dirt invoice. This procedure allowed for later substitution of inflated weight tickets by the dirt contractor.

As there was no proper internal control on the flow of the paper work, Chester felt that there was margin for fraud, meaning that the plant was probably being overcharged for the actual volume of dirt being delivered.

The Dirty Deal

Chester returned to the car and told Clyde that he believed there was a good possibility that the plant was being overcharged and gave the reasons for his suspicions.

As they were scheduled to leave for another job that night, Clyde said, "Well, to prove what you think would take the auditors several days to document and confirm your suspicions. We can either get the auditors involved and come back in a couple weeks or we can take a short cut."

Chester asked Clyde what he had in mind.

Clyde said, "Come on, let's drive down to the trucking contractors main office."

When they arrived, they asked to see the company owner.

They went into the owner's office and introduced themselves.

Clyde said, "We've been checking out your truck dirt deliveries. We don't know whether you are involved in the overcharges or if it's just your truck drivers acting on their own. We are on our way down to the Commonwealth Attorney's Office. Out of courtesy to you, we stopped by to see if you want to go with us."

The astonished owner said he didn't have any idea what we were talking about.

As we headed for the door, Clyde said, "Well fine, we will just be on our way to the Commonwealth Attorney's Office.

The owner said, "Wait!" He said, "I'm not aware of any dirt overcharges, but if you think there is a problem, how much do you think you have been overcharged?"

Clyde, looking at Chester, replied, "He's the financial man but he told me he thought the loss was about $65,421.65. Right Chester?"

Chester said, "That sounds about right."

The owner then said, "Gosh I didn't think it was that much. Can you prove that amount?"

Clyde said, "We can."

The owner then replied, "If you can prove the amount you say you were overcharged and I pay back your purported loss, will you forget about going to the Commonwealth Attorney's Office?"

Clyde said, "I'll tell you what, you come by the plant tonight with a cashiers check and we will show you our records proving the loss. You can then give us the check when you are satisfied with the records and we will agree not to go to the prosecutor's office.

In addition your people and our plant auditors will meet to agree on a new procedure to guarantee this doesn't happen again.

The owner agreed.

As they got in the car, Clyde turned to Chester and said, "How are you going to prove the loss?"

Chester replied, "Gee thanks Clyde. I don't have any idea."

They went to the plant. They had about two hours before the owner would arrive. Chester got out several legal file folders and filled them with blank yellow 21 column working papers. He headed the first few pages with truck identification numbers as he had seen on the side of the trucks entering the plant. Down the sides of the pages, Chester placed dates corresponding with the dates of the truck dirt deliveries.

Down the columns he placed truck weight numbers representing dirt deliveries.

Chester then started running an adding machine tape supposedly representing the amount of loss per truck as shown on the fabricated working papers. The total of the tape was made to correspond with the amount of money Clyde told the owner represented the overcharges.

Just as Chester placed four legal sized files on the desk, the trucking firm owner arrived.

Clyde told the owner to come over to the desk and Chester would show him the loss calculations.

Chester hurriedly opened one of the file folders and showed how he had listed the trucks by delivery date with the loss amount indicated by each truck. The adding machine tape attached equaled the aggregate loss.

Chester then hurriedly closed the folders and pushed them aside before the owner had time to get a good look at them.

The owner exclaimed, "Damn, you do have the proof don't you."

He handed Chester the check and left.

That night the chairman of the board of the parent company flew into the airport in his private airplane to pick up Clyde and Chester to return them home.

They told the CEO about the recoveries that had been made that day feeling very proud of what they had done.

The Dirty Deal

The CEO told them, "Hell you aren't so smart. You probably left three times that amount of money on the table. Why else do you think he so readily agreed to pay you"?

Clyde and Chester's ego had just been royally deflated.

PIPELINES, OIL AND GAS, CONVENIENCE STORES

THE CRUDE OIL AND THE DEEP FREEZE CASE

While conducting an audit of a farming operation on the west coast, Chester overheard employees from the company's adjoining oil and gas production and exploration division office talking about three oil strikes recently made in which each oil well was producing 1,000 barrels of oil per day.

Being curious and not having previously seen on-shore oil wells this prolific, Chester later asked to see the last two months daily production reports for these wells.

In reviewing these reports, Chester noted that daily production was averaging about 925, 933, 941, 1,008, 921, 934 and 1,009 barrels of oil per day per well each week.

Chester mentioned to the production manager that it appeared they didn't actually have 1,000 barrel a day wells.

The production manager told Chester he just didn't understand the oil business. Chester was told that the gaugers and pumpers don't always check production at the same time each day. Therefore, that accounts for the wells not showing 1,000 barrels each day.

Chester retorted with, "If that is so why doesn't it average out to 1,000 barrels every two or three days?"

Chester again was told that he just didn't understand the oil business.

Chester then asked, "How do you measure well production?"

Chester was told that each well had a pipeline running to a three-tank battery collection system. All oil was pumped into one tank until it was filled. Then a float shut off production to that tank and oil production was switched to the next empty tank. Production of the wells was measured by the amount of oil in the tanks each morning less the amounts shipped during the past day.

Chester was told that oil tanker trucks came by periodically to load oil out of only the full tanks. The trucks then transported and unloaded the oil into a refinery pipeline header located about a mile and a half down the road.

The refinery pipeline transported the oil about ten miles to a local refinery. The company was paid on the basis of oil delivery tickets prepared by the transport truck drivers and subsequently forwarded to the local refinery for payment to customers.

Chester then asked the production manager what was to prevent the truckers from loading out of one of the tanks that was not full but into which production was currently being pumped.

The Crude Oil And The Deep Freeze Case

Chester was told that this couldn't happen as the valves locked in such a manner that oil could only be unloaded from a full tank.

This story did not make a lot of sense to Chester so that afternoon he told Clyde of his findings and conversations.

That evening they drove out to the tank battery to see just how the system worked. They climbed up on the walkway to each tank and observed the oil flowing into one of the tanks.

They then checked the valves on the unloading dock and discovered oil could be run out of either of the three tanks whether the tanks were full or not.

As two of the tanks were full, they presumed a truck might come by that evening to take product.

They drove their rental car behind some scrubs and waited. In about an hour an oil transport truck arrived and began filling up with oil.

After filling the truck with oil, the driver drove down the road to the refinery pipeline header to unload.

They followed. They observed that the driver hooked up the hose lines from the truck to the pipeline header and then got back into the truck.

After about forty-five minutes the driver got out of the truck and began unhooking the hose lines. Then he got back into the truck and drove off.

They noted that the driver was changing gears so often it was obvious that the trucks tank was still full of oil.

The truck was followed about twenty miles across the backcountry roads until it came to an abandoned tank battery where the oil was unloaded.

Having noted the name of the trucking firm on the side of the truck, they drove to the trucking firm office and asked to see the owner.

As it was then about 10:00 pm in the evening, the owner was at home. The owner was telephoned and told that there was a serious problem. He was requested to come to his office.

At this point, it was not known whether the owner and truck drivers were conspiring together to steal crude oil or if truckers were operating alone.

Investigating Corporate Fraud

Clyde confronted the owner with the information we had gathered. The owner convinced Clyde that he knew nothing about the matter. The owner stated that if crude oil was being stolen it was by truck drivers without his knowledge.

They decided to wait for the observed truck driver to return to the trucking firm office. When the driver arrived Clyde took him into the office and confronted him with the information they had obtained.

After denying any involvement, the driver later changed his story and gave Clyde a signed statement in which he admitted the oil thefts.

The truck driver not only admitted his involvement in the oil thefts from the company but also stated that many truckers were stealing oil from all the other oil producers in the area. All the truckers were working together to get rich.

The truck driver then took Clyde and Chester to his home. There he opened his long lowboy deep freeze that was full of packaged one hundred dollar bills he had saved from his thefts. There were thousands and thousands of dollars in the freezer. The money was confiscated pending the outcome of the investigation.

As they were interested in cleaning up all the oil thefts in the area, they convinced the driver to meet with security personnel from all other oil producers operating in the area. At the meeting, the driver promised to point out on an area map all of the tank batteries from which oil was being stolen. The driver was promised prosecution leniency for cooperating.

The next day, Chester called the refinery office and asked how much crude oil line loss they were experiencing. He was told that the line loss averaged about seven to eight percent.

Chester told them he thought that amount was impossible unless they had a large leak somewhere in the line.

He was told that they did not have an oil leak in the line and were satisfied with the percentage of loss being normal.

Chester checked the company's records and discovered the company was being paid for the crude oil the truck driver had stolen. Apparently, paper work covering the amount of oil stolen and not unloaded into the pipeline was being forwarded to the refinery for payment.

The refinery paid the company based on the fraudulent delivery paper work. The crude oil being diverted was apparently showing up in the refinery crude oil pipeline loss figures.

The Crude Oil And The Deep Freeze Case

A few days later, security personnel from other oil companies in the area attended a meeting at which time the truck driver pointed out on an area map all the wells and tank batteries from which crude oil was being stolen. The security personnel advised Chester and Clyde that they were unaware of any crude oil thefts from their company's wells but would go back to their home office and later advise their findings.

Surprisingly, a week or so later they were advised by the security personnel who attended the meeting that their companies were not incurring any field crude oil production loss.

This was puzzling. As this was the time that the Federal Government had in place a three tier crude oil pricing schedule for oil production, they could only conclude that the oil companies and the refinery might be playing games with their crude oil classifications in order to receive higher payments for crude oil than allowed by Federal Government Regulations. Therefore they did not want to get involved in any investigation that might result in their criminal prosecution for fraud.

As the company had not lost any money and the other oil companies in the area would not acknowledge any loss, they knew prosecution of the driver was not possible. The money was returned to him that had obtained from his freezer.

Their investigation did result in breaking up the crude oil trucker's theft ring.

THE ROSE AND THE PAPER SACK

The company was spending a substantial amount of money in drilling offshore oil and gas wells. Only two major contractors were available and capable of supplying the personnel and equipment necessary to carry out the offshore drilling requirements. Many other companies were used to obtain oil field supplies and services.

A high-ranking officer employed by the company supervised the company's drilling program and contract administration.

Company auditors became suspicious when rumors surfaced in the industry that kickbacks by oil field service companies to customer employees were common. They also heard rumors that a top company executive had some sort of deal with the offshore drilling contractors

Clyde and Chester were called in to investigate these rumors.

The investigation covered a three-state area. Several frauds were discovered where oil field suppliers gave the company's employees kickbacks in order to gain business.

In one of the cities where many oil companies operated, a supplier had set up a four bedroom house trailer at the edge of town that was kept well supplied with food, liquor, and women available to clients and customers twenty four hours a day.

Several of the company's employees were fired and prosecuted for frauds uncovered during the investigation. However, no one would offer any information or comments about the high-ranking officer who had become a target of the investigation. They all seemed afraid to talk in fear of loosing their jobs.

Interviews with other suppliers in the area produced no tangible information.

Chester began a background check into the net worth of the executive. Property records were reviewed in fifteen area county courthouses.

Information gathered from deed records and other sources disclosed the net worth of the executive had increased over $2,000,000 during the prior three years.

Although the executive earned a good salary, he did not earn enough salary and benefits to have acquired even a portion of the assets acquired.

Information obtained disclosed extensive common stock holdings, a ranch, ranch house, oil field rod fencing, cattle guards, horse barns, cattle, horses, and other items.

When no one would talk or provide any information pertinent to the investigation, Clyde and Chester felt that they had exhausted about all their resources.

Then they learned that the Justice Department and the Internal Revenue Service were investigating the two drilling contractors. Contacts with the appropriate agencies were made and information exchanged.

Federal investigations disclosed that the two companies, in addition to making payoffs to the company's high-ranking executive, were also dividing up the offshore business and protecting each other on contract bids. This resulted in one contractor getting all the business east of a north south line and the other contractor all business on the west side. Obviously, this practice resulted in overcharges to all the contractor's customers including the company.

Upon completion of the Federal investigation, the two drilling contractors contacted the company. They offered to provide all information about their improper business dealings with the company including kickbacks made to the executive.

Clyde and Chester had been unable to obtain any pertinent information in their investigation because the deal struck by the company's executive was made at such a high level in the drilling contractors office that no one else had any facts or first hand knowledge of the fraudulent transaction.

Information provided by the drilling contractors disclosed that the executive was getting a kickback equal to about 2% to 3% of the total amount the company spent on drilling contracts. The company employee had received over $ 2,000,000 in kickbacks over several years. The contractors not only charged the company for the amount of the kickbacks but substantially more.

The arrangements that the executive had made with the drilling contractors to receive his payoff sounded like something out of a mystery novel.

The executive called a high-ranking officer with the drilling contractors when he wanted to pick up some money. He made arrangements to appear at a prominent London, England hotel at 10:00 am on a designated day wearing a red rose in the lapel of a dark blue suit. He stood by the check-in counter. An employee from the drilling company approached the executive at the designated time and place and gave him a paper sack filled with $100 bills. This exchange took place on many occasions over several years.

The executive then laundered the money through Mexico into the United States with the intent of hiding the income from the Internal Revenue Service.

The Internal Revenue Service pursued prosecution of the executive and confiscation of his assets.

The company initiated appropriate action against the drilling contractors to recover the amount of the kickbacks plus other overcharges.

EQUIPPING THE RANCH

When rumors of kickbacks in an out of state oil patch came to the attention of the company, Clyde and Chester were requested to investigate the supplier companies used by the company in that area of operation.

Chester reviewed the purchasing records to determine which companies the client used for acquiring materials and service in the identified area.

They began interviewing supplier company personnel. Each was told that the client did not approve nor sanction giving kickbacks to the company's employees in order to gain business.

Obviously, if kickbacks were given to employees, the supplier companies had to increase their prices in order to recapture the cost of the kickbacks given those employees. Each supplier was also asked if they found the client's bid practices for services and supplies fair.

Interviews were also conducted with supplier companies that had not received business from the client. Some of the suppliers indicated they were not allowed on the bid list as they refused to give kickbacks to the company's employees.

During the course of the interviews, one supplier admitted to having given several head of cattle to a manager in the company's local office. The supplier had purchased 6 cows and a bull. A truck had also been engaged to deliver the livestock to the manager's ranch located about 70 miles away. Clyde took a statement from the supplier's employee detailing this transaction.

After getting similar information from several other suppliers, they went to the company's office in the area and confronted the manager.

Clyde obtained a signed statement from the manager in which he admitted having received as kick-backs from various suppliers a tractor, barn, 70 head of cattle, labor and materials for construction of a small ranch house, stove, refrigerator, deep freeze, fencing, cattle guards, road work, hay and many other items of use in equipping his ranch and ranch house. The value of all these items was estimated to be in excess of $185,000.

The man was terminated and turned over to the police for prosecution.

The company completely revised all purchasing policies and bid procedures.

Based on information gained from the investigation, the company was able to recover about $78,000 in restitution from the supplier companies that had given kick backs to the company's former employees. The company bore the balance of the loss as the loss did not exceed the fidelity insurance bond deductible.

Investigating Corporate Fraud

THE STOLEN OFFICE EQUIPMENT AND DRUGS

A local oil company was experiencing thefts of typewriters, adding machines and calculators. Clyde and Chester were requested to investigate.

The equipment was apparently being taken at night after all the employees had gone home.

That night they set up a surveillance of the office area in an attempt to catch someone coming into the building after everyone had left. About eight that night a man entered the office area, looked around, and sat down at his desk. They observed the man for a while. He appeared to be working on some papers. The man was approached and they determined that he was an employee. The man appeared very nervous and looked guilty of something. Clyde confronted him about the thefts of equipment but he denied any knowledge of the thefts.

Clyde used a local lie detector firm as an investigative tool under some circumstances. Arrangements had been previously made to have an operator on hand that night if needed.

The employee continually denied any involvement in any thefts and agreed to take a lie detector test to prove his innocence.

Chester asked the employee to go with him to the testing building. As the client's office was on the second floor of the building, Chester and the employee approached the elevator. When the door opened, they both got on the elevator. Just before the elevator door closed, the suspect jumped off. When the elevator reached the first floor, Chester got off and ran up the stairway in case the employee was trying to run. But the employee was standing at the elevator and stated that he had forgotten something and had just returned to his desk to retrieve the item.

When the operator had finished the test, he advised Chester that the polygraph had virtually deadlined as the employee evidently had taken a drug, which nullified his emotions. Therefore the test was worthless. As the suspect had been out of Chester's sight for a couple minutes at the office, he apparently had used that time to take some type of drug.

The employee was advised that the test was inconclusive and he was sent home.

Chester met Clyde the next morning and told Clyde of the events of the prior evening. Chester told him that the employee was obviously involved in something illegal but wasn't talking yet.

They went back to the client company's office the next day, brought the employee into the office and interrogated him again. Since he was apparently on drugs the night before they worked on that angle. The employee eventually admitted to having stolen office equipment and sold the items for money to acquire drugs. He also stated that his girl friend worked at a local hospital and was stealing drugs there. Some of the drugs they used to satisfy their drug habit and the rest was sold. These details were reduced to a signed statement of admission. The employee was terminated and turned over to the police.

They approached management at a local hospital and asked if they were missing any drugs. A review disclosed that the hospital's control over their drug inventory was very loose. The hospital management admitted to having incurred loss of drugs but could not estimate the amount. The girl friend was interviewed at the hospital and finally admitted her involvement in the drug thefts. She was terminated and also turned over to the police.

No recovery could be made of the losses incurred by the client and hospital.

WHO GOT THE ROYALTIES?

Clyde and Chester were requested to investigate a company's land lease acquisition program when a district office employee noticed that several unknown company names started appearing as royalty owners on newly acquired land leases.

The district office employed several field land men to approach landowners in the area to seek an oil and gas lease on their lands.

The landowners were approached usually for a three-year lease that allowed the company to drill on their land for oil and gas. The landowner in most cases retained a 15% to 20% royalty interest in any and all oil and gas produced from wells subsequently drilled on the property.

In the last six months, several names unknown to the company began showing up on the land leases with a 1% to 1 1/2% royalty interest in addition to the usual landowner's royalty interest.

The division office reported this information to the home office that then requested an investigation be initiated by Clyde and Chester.

Upon arriving at the client's district office, they began reviewing the leases and listing the company names on the leases with the minority royalty interest.

Corporate records were checked with the secretary of state as well as county records for corporate and assumed names to determine ownership of the new companies.

This review disclosed that several companies had been organized by one of the field land men employed by the company's district office. This land man was conveying royalty interests to his own personal companies.

As the field land man was in another city that day seeking land leases, they went there to locate him. That evening the man was confronted at his motel room when he returned from the field.

Clyde began interrogating the man about his activities and he eventually admitted that he had set up several companies for use in assigning royalty interests in effect to himself. He felt that the leases covered very good oil and gas prospects and planned to earn a lot of income over the subsequent years through this fraud. A signed statement was obtained from the land man. He was also convinced to sign all his company's interests in the oil and gas royalties over to his employer. As of that date no oil or gas wells had yet been drilled on the leases.

The field land man was then terminated. The company decided not to pursue prosecution.

PISTOL IN THE SKY

When a convenience store operation in Miami suffered a substantial cash shortage, Clyde and Chester were requested to investigate.

They flew in the company's private airplane to Miami to determine the amount of the loss and how it occurred.

After checking cash receipts and deposits at three convenience stores, they determined that about $43,000 had been taken one evening.

An area supervisor came by each store at night and picked up the cash and check receipts for the day. He then made a drop at a bank night depository. However, when he picked up $43,000 for deposit from the three stores one night, he apparently took the money and disappeared from the city.

Checking employment applications, they learned that the former area supervisor had a sister who lived on Long Island in New York.

The man was divorced and his two children were living with the sister.

They surmised that the area supervisor had fled to New York to his sister's house thinking that no one would bother to follow him there for his return to Miami for prosecution.

Checking criminal records, they learned that the man had been booked three times for assault but only prosecuted once. He was a large, muscular black man, reportedly with a very bad temper.

The convenience store management had not conducted a background check before hiring him.

Clyde and Chester took the airplane to New York in pursuit of the former area supervisor.

Arriving at the sister's house, Clyde told Chester to wait in the car while he tried to persuade the man to return to Miami.

Clyde knocked on the door. The sister came to the door and Clyde asked to speak to her brother. She seemed surprised, as she didn't think anyone knew he was there.

The former area supervisor came to the door. Clyde identified himself.

Pistol In The Sky

As the man was eating breakfast, Clyde invited himself in and asked to join him in a cup of coffee. While making small talk, Clyde was trying to figure how to con the man into returning to Miami.

At first, when approached with the theft, the man denied any involvement. In any case, he wasn't going back to Miami.

Clyde finally convinced him that if he went back to Miami now and turned himself in to the Miami police, Clyde would see that he got a minimum jail sentence. Otherwise, if the Miami police had to track him down and take him back, he could expect to receive the maximum jail sentence.

After thinking the situation over, the former employee finally agreed to return to Miami. He went into the bedroom, packed his gear, and left the house with Clyde.

They all returned to the airport and flew to Miami. Chester had called ahead and ordered plenty of food to eat on the way back in order to make the trip as pleasant as possible. Obviously, the liquor cabinet remained locked.

About half way to Miami, the man suddenly pulled out a 38-caliber pistol and started waving it in the air. He said, "I think I've changed my mind. I don't want to go back to Miami after all."

Clyde and the man were sitting directly across the aisle from and facing Chester. Neither Clyde nor Chester had any idea what the man would do next. They certainly didn't want a gun to be fired in the airplane.

Clyde asked, "What are you going to do with the gun?"

He replied, "I don't know yet."

Chester cautioned, "Don't let the pilots see that pistol or they may do something crazy."

Clyde then asked, "When did you get the pistol?"

The man replied, "I got it before we left New York when I was packing my bag."

Finally, Chester held out his hand and said, "Why don't you give me the pistol. I'll hide it under the seat. You don't want to get in trouble with the Feds when we land."

Surprisingly, the man handed Chester the gun and said, "I guess you are right."

Clyde and Chester both sighed inwardly in relief. The rest of the trip was thankfully uneventful.

The pilots had been instructed to call ahead to request Miami police to meet the airplane upon arrival. When the airplane landed, the Miami police picked up the former employee and took him to jail.

Clyde got rid of the pistol so there would be no more trouble.

They never knew why the pistol was brought on board or what use the man had in mind for it. They never told the pilots about the incident.

True to his word, Clyde saw that the man got only a minimum sentence for cooperating with them.

The company's loss of $43,000 was recovered from the filing of a fidelity bond insurance claim.

THE STOLEN MAPS

The company was engaged in the exploration and production of oil and gas. In the course of determining which areas would be drilled, geological and geophysical studies were made. Many geophysical maps were prepared covering the company's acreage.

The company approached Clyde with information that an employee had given a competitor company employee some of the company's geophysical maps.

The employee apparently was either seeking employment with the competitor or setting himself up to sell maps to that company in the future.

The company advised that the maps given to the competitor were old and covered acreage the Company was no longer interested in exploring.

Clyde suggested approaching the competitor company and visit with their employee who was given the geophysical maps. The company agreed and the competitor company was approached and agreed that their employee be interviewed.

Clyde interviewed the competitor's employee to determine his relationship with the company's employee. Clyde found out that the parties had met at a local oil and gas convention and were not necessarily good friends.

Clyde asked the man if he would approach the company's employee to see if he would sell current geophysical maps to him. The man agreed.

The next time they met, the competitor's employee asked the company's employee if he had any more maps for him. The company's employee said that he didn't have any now but that he could get some more if the money was right.

He was asked how much he needed. He was told that he could get some maps if he could get at least $10,000.

The men made a deal to get together the following week at a specified location.

The competitor's employee telephoned Clyde. He reported that he was going to meet the company's employee to receive maps but that he wanted $10,000.

Clyde told him that he would provide the $10,000 just before the meeting. Clyde wanted to wait in the adjoining room to overhear and tape the conversations.

On the specified date, the competitor's employee and Clyde went to the designated location. Clyde waited in the next room.

The Stolen Maps

The company's employee arrived at the meeting with a roll of maps under his arm. He asked for the $10,000 and the man handed it to him.

As he was counting the money, Clyde stepped into the room and confronted him with stealing the company's property. As he was caught red handed, he willingly gave Clyde a signed statement covering his fraudulent activity.

The maps were recovered and returned to the company. The maps again turned out to be old and of no use to either the company or competitor.

Since the maps were of no apparent use to anyone, the company's employee was terminated and no criminal charges were pursued.

THE BUGS

Chester and Clyde had just finished an investigation in the northeast and were ready to head home. The CEO of the company requested that they stop by Washington D. C. on the way. He wanted them to check the office area and telephones to be sure there were no bugging devices.

Years ago company pipeline personnel were in D. C. to present an application to the Federal Power Commission that approved pipeline construction and rates charged gas customers. A competitor company was there for the same purpose of obtaining approval for a new pipeline.

Each evening company personnel would gather in a meeting room in their hotel to plan for the next day's presentation. The next day when the meeting took place the competitor seemed to know in advance what the company was going to present and had prepared to refute their presentation. This was very disturbing.

Clyde was called to go through the company's hotel and meeting rooms to check for bugging devices. Bugs were found in the meeting room and hotel rooms including the company CEO's room. It was obvious that the competitor company had caused the bugs to be installed. The company's CEO was furious. He called the competitor's CEO and told him that he was going to advise the governmental agency of their illegal activities. In addition, press releases would be made that could also arouse the competitor's stockholders. The CEO of the competitor company apologized profusely and said that his company would withdraw their application immediately if the matter could be dropped, which it was.

From that time forward, certain of the home office telephones and offices in Washington D.C. were debugged periodically.

The company CEO wanted Clyde and Chester to stop by Washington and debug the office and phones on the way home. They were told to land in D.C. around six o'clock and send the company plane on to Virginia to wait until they were ready to leave. The executive wanted them to slip into the office after everyone was gone for the day. He didn't want anyone to know they had been there.

They completed their review and Clyde called the executive about 11 o'clock that night to report the findings. The executive repeated his wish that they get in and out of D.C. without anyone having knowledge of them being there. He advised that the pilots wouldn't be happy but call them in Virginia to bring the plane to pick them up now and head for home. Chester called the pilots and woke them up in their hotel room and told them what the executive had instructed. The pilots rushed the plane out of Virginia to the Dulles airport where Clyde and Chester were waiting.

The Bugs

On company flights Clyde and Chester always waited on the pilots bringing them coffee, juice, sandwiches, etc. Chester talked to one of the pilots and only got grunts out of him. The pilot wouldn't say a word on the way home. He obviously was mad.

When they arrived home in early morn, Chester asked the other pilot what was the problem. He advised that the pilot had just gotten married and had been on his honeymoon prior to this trip. In the rush to get out of Virginia, the pilot had left his false teeth in a glass in the bathroom. He was so embarrassed, especially going home without his teeth.

Chester told the pilot that one of the men in his office was in the same motel in Virginia waiting to attend an early meeting that morning. Chester would call now, wake him up, and ask him to go to the pilot's room now before the maids would be there. He was asked to get the pilots teeth and bring them home with him later on in that day, which he did.

The pilot was glad to get his teeth back as he was tired of gumming it.

INSURANCE

THE INSURANCE SCAM

The company owed an insurance company primarily in the business of writing life insurance policies.

The company had issued a policy about two months before on the life of an individual in the amount of $100,000. The beneficiary was the man's wife.

The company got word that the man had been shot several times while in a local motel room. Information obtained disclosed that a rifle fired through the outside wall of the motel had killed the man. For some strange reason, the death had been ruled a suicide.

Clyde and Chester were requested to review the matter before the $100,000 face value of the policy was paid to the beneficiary.

Beginning the investigation, they determined that the man and his wife had been married only a week or two before the life insurance policy had been purchased. This seemed strange.

A background check on the wife was made. Information obtained disclosed that the woman had been married three times in the past year and in each instance her new husband had been killed shortly after an insurance policy had been taken out on his life.

They interviewed the widow in an attempt to find out any information that might be relevant. She appeared to be very frightened and wouldn't reveal any information. She said she planned to file a formal claim against the policy and expected to be paid.

She was advised to go ahead and file the claim but that the insurance company, under the circumstances, was not going to pay the claim.

She was told that her recourse was to sue the company for the money. This would give the Company an opportunity to take her deposition and also cross exam her on the witness stand during the court trial. This information seemed to further frighten her. She said that she wasn't sure now if she still wanted to file a claim for the money.

In checking with other insurance companies, they learned that many had been hit with claims on policies under the same set of circumstances.

Several companies had paid out double the face value of the insurance policies as they covered double indemnity on accidental death claims.

It was rumored that the Mexican Mafia in the Dallas area had organized several women whose purpose was to target men who they could convince to marry them. Shortly after marriage, insurance policies were taken out on their husband's lives.

The Insurance Scam

Usually, within a week or two thereafter, these men would be suddenly killed.

Since most of the insurance companies had been paying the claims, the scam was being continued with the policies rotated between different insurance companies.

Clyde knew someone in Las Vegas that might have a contact with the Mexican Mafia, assuming it existed. Clyde and Chester went to Las Vegas to review the matter with the possible contact.

They met with a manager of one of the major casinos. They thought he might be able to help. They discussed their findings and advised that their company would not pay such claims without being taken to court and forced to pay.

They suggested that if such a scam was being perpetrated, perhaps he could advise the Mexican Mafia that the company was going to fight in court any such claims against them.

The casino manager said he didn't know anything about the Mexican Mafia but that he would ask around.

Clyde and Chester assumed their message was relayed, as the claim was never filed for the $100,000 policy they had investigated. The company incurred no other such claims.

If the fraud continued to be perpetuated, it was with insurance companies other than the company.

REAL ESTATE

Investigating Corporate Fraud

THE SAFE DEPOSIT BOX

A construction company was engaged in building apartment projects and remodeling motels.

The construction superintendent was responsible for supervising the overall performance of the work. In addition, he was responsible for buying all of the lumber and materials used on the construction project. He had worked for the company for several years and was thought to be a valuable and trusted employee.

The superintendent was not married and lived with his mother. He was an avid motorcyclist. He loved to ride his motorcycle across the country and seldom was seen in an automobile.

One evening after work, he was riding out through the countryside when he lost control of the motorcycle, ran off the road into a tree, and was killed.

A vice-president of the construction company was a close personal friend of the deceased. He assisted the mother in handling all of the financial affairs in processing the estate.

During this assistance, the vice-president went with the mother to the bank where the construction superintendent had conducted his financial affairs.

In the course of completing business at the bank, one of the bank officers reminded the mother that her son had maintained a safe deposit box at the bank.

When the mother decided to inventory and empty the safe deposit box, she asked the vice-president of the company to go with her to inventory the contents.

Upon opening the box, to the mother's surprise, she found among the papers a stack of neatly wrapped $100 bills. When counted, there was a total of $60,000. The mother said she had no idea how her son could have saved so much money.

After leaving the bank and returning to the construction office, the vice-president began thinking about how his friend could have accumulated that much money.

Although not suspecting any fraud in the matter, he decided to ask Clyde and Chester to conduct an audit and investigation of that portion of business handled by the construction superintendent.

Chester began a review of the major lumber purchases made during the past two years. Prices paid were compared to prices available from other sources on the same materials.

The Safe Deposit Box

Upon completing this review, Chester noted that prices paid were about 10% higher than prices available from several other sources. The lumber and material overcharges amounted to about $70,000.

Clyde went to the lumberyards where the construction materials had been purchased to interview people handling the lumber and material sales to the company.

When approached with the information gathered in the price comparisons, personnel at the lumberyards admitted to having paid the construction superintendent a 10% kickback in order to obtain the business.

Clyde obtained signed statements covering their improprieties.

They presented the information obtained to the vice-president. He was devastated by their findings.

As the construction company had in force a fidelity bond insurance policy covering its employees, Chester prepared, filed, and collected an insurance claim for the $70,000 loss to the client company.

The company's vice president didn't want to confront the deceased employees' mother that the $ 60,000 found in the safe deposit box was obtained by fraud. As that couldn't be proved, nothing was said. The mother kept the money found in the box.

MISUSING THE COMPANY LABOR

One of the executives of a company was in the process of building a new house on his ranch located about 100 miles from the city.

The company's real estate division had employees that provided electrical and other construction labor in the remodeling of company offices and retail rentals.

The company executive requested that company electrical and construction employees assist in the wiring, plumbing and construction of his ranch house as he thought that company-remodeling work was slow at that time.

During the course of the performance of this work, the employees bought various materials and supplies that were charged to the company.

While this work was progressing, a company employee told Chester of rumors that company employees were performing work at the executive's ranch that was not company related.

Chester requested a meeting with the executive and advised him of the rumors. The executive confirmed that work indeed was being performed by company employees, but that he didn't think anything was wrong, as their supervisor had advised that he didn't have any work for them to do anyway at that time.

The executive was asked if he ever thought that the supervisor might just be trying to ingratiate himself with the executive.

He stated, "I had not thought about it but that was entirely possible."

Chester said that if the executive didn't mind, he would like to talk to the real estate supervisor. The executive agreed.

Chester interviewed the supervisor of the employees performing the work. The supervisor advised that he agreed to provide the employees to perform the work as he was afraid if he didn't he might receive repercussions later from the executive.

The supervisor stated that he was not aware that the employees were charging materials and supplies to the company while performing the work.

Chester met again with the executive and advised him of the discussions with the supervisor. The executive asked Chester, "What shall I do?"

Chester advised that using company employees on his personal work sent a bad signal to the rest of the employees, as it had become general knowledge what was taking

Misusing The Company Labor

place. The employees would obviously think that if it was all right for the executive to use company labor and materials, they should be able to do so as well.

The executive was advised that the proper thing would be for Chester to prepare an invoice for him covering the actual cost to the company for the man-hours and materials used on the ranch project.

The executive agreed.

Chester prepared an invoice covering $65,000 in company labor, benefits and materials incurred in connection with the work at the ranch. The invoice was submitted to the executive who immediately made payment to reimburse the company.

THE GUARD WHO SHOT STRAIGHT

In another case, we introduced you to our friend Al. He owned and managed a security guard service. He had a contract covering guard services at a high-rise downtown hotel-parking garage.

Clyde and Chester were responsible for the guards providing a similar service for the hotel and two buildings across the street. The company owned an interest in both of the buildings.

One evening several men drove a car into the hotel parking garage and left their car. They went up to the revolving bar at the top of the hotel for a few drinks.

Leaving the bar rather drunk after midnight, they returned to their car and drove to the exit to pay their parking ticket.

One of Al's armed guards was on duty. The driver of the car could not find his parking ticket. Rather than charging the driver the maximum of $6, the guard argued with the driver about the ticket. The guard told the driver he couldn't leave the garage without a parking ticket.

The driver put the car in gear and drove out of the garage through the security arm and turned onto the one-way street headed the wrong way.

The guard drew his gun and ran out onto the street firing four or five shots into the back of the car. Fortunately, no one in the car was hit by any of the bullets.

Although the men in the car were drunk, having the rear of their car fired into must have sobered them. They promptly drove to the police station and reported the incident.

About 7 o'clock the next morning when Chester arrived at the office, a guard in the company's office building reported the incident to him.

Chester went to the parking garage to find out the details. He learned that Al's guard who was involved in the incident had gone off duty at 7 o'clock that morning. The guard reportedly lived in the Far East side of town and usually stopped in a neighborhood bar for a couple of beers on his way home.

Chester was concerned that the car occupants might try and drag the hotel and office building into any actions taken against Al's company.

Chester located Al's guard in the bar and questioned him about the incident. The guard gave Chester a signed statement in which he admitted having fired shots into the car.

He said, "I was just angry with the way the occupants of the car had treated me."

Chester asked, "Where did you get the pistol?"

The guard said, "I was just walking through Al's office one day when he handed me a pistol and told me to wear it on duty."

He told Chester he had never before fired a pistol. The guard service gave him no instructions on what he was to do with the gun. He had received no training in the use of firearms. The guard had worked for Al about two months. He had never worn a side arm on his previous employer's guard jobs.

Chester knew Al was going to be in trouble over this incident and decided to have some fun with him. Arriving back at the office, Chester called Al to see if he knew about the incident. Al said he had just learned about it. Chester told Al he had better come down to Clyde's office as it sounded like he was in big trouble.

Clyde was shown the statement taken by Chester and they waited for Al to arrive.

They showed Al the statement and asked, "Al what are you going to do about the people in the car?"

He replied, "I'm not going to do anything until I hear from someone."

They chided Al telling him, "That is just great. In the meantime the police will be looking for you and the guard."

Al got angry with them and said, "Thanks a lot. You guys sure put me in the grease."

Chester told Al, "Your guard is the one that put you in the grease. I won't be surprised if you get sued big time over this incident."

Al asked Chester, "Why in the world did you take a statement from my guard?"

They kidded Al and told him, "Someone has to look after your business while you sleep all morning."

Al asked, "What should I do?"

Chester told him, "If it was me, I would find out right now who owned the car and offer to buy him a new car if no charges or lawsuits are pursued."

Al replied, "I can't afford that."

Chester told Al, "You can't afford not to."

Clyde told Al, "Check with your insurance agent as your insurance might cover the incident."

Al grumbled as he left Clyde's office. They had gotten the best of Al again.

But, Al took their advice and bought the driver a new car. No charges were pursued against Al, his guard company, or the guard. Hopefully, Al had learned a lesson pertaining to the use of armed guards.

WHAT HAPPENED TO THE RENT?

A company owned considerable real estate property. The properties were concentrated in about three different adjacent areas in the state.

The company had acquired several thousand acres just outside a college town. The company knew that a new freeway was going to be built along the front of its properties that would facilitate commercial development.

The company had acquired the land in a series of purchases of adjacent farms that had family residences on the property.

The residences on the properties had been rented pending commercial development that would not occur for a couple more years. The company had hired a man to rent the houses and collect the applicable rent each month.

As vacancy rates had risen consistently during the past several months, the company became suspicious. Clyde and Chester were contacted to investigate.

They went to the area where the farms and rent houses were located. They went from house to house to determine if they were occupied.

In most instances, the homes reported vacant were in fact occupied.

They questioned the occupants about their rental payments. In each case, the occupants produced rental receipts provided by the company's employee at the time rent was paid.

After completing the interviews, they found that the company's employee had diverted about $17,000 in rental receipts to his own personal use.

Clyde confronted the employee with their findings. The employee finally admitted that he had stolen the rental receipts and gave Clyde a signed confession.

The company employee had falsified his monthly rental reports submitted to the company's office. The reports reflected the property vacant when in fact the houses continued to be rented. The company's employee had pocketed the rent money collected.

The man was terminated. The client did not wish to prosecute.

AGRICULTURE AND CONSTRUCTION EQUIPMENT

THE DISAPPEARING BATTERIES

The company had just acquired a corporation that had numerous agricultural manufacturing facilities and wanted a review of the major assembly plant operations primarily aimed at possible fraud.

Clyde and Chester arrived on the scene and began reviewing various areas of plant operations.

Chester began by reviewing the employment files covering employees recently hired. He noted that persons currently housed in federal penitentiaries submitted many employment applications. Many of these individuals had subsequently been hired.

Background checks revealed that most of these individuals had been in prison on drug-related charges.

After reviewing this information with Clyde, they speculated several of these employees were probably stealing plant parts, materials and supplies for sale to cover drug habits.

The company's auditors were asked to review purchases and inventory records for the past two years for three major items used in the manufacturing process; tires, batteries, and radios.

Chester hoped that the auditors could provide them with information relative to possible inventory shortages.

While on various reviews, they often pulled pranks on each other.

It was a cold February. A couple of feet of snow was on the ground. They had made friends with the cashier at the hotel where they stayed.

The cashier looked like a fabled TV undertaker actor so they nicknamed him 'Digger O'Dell.'

On the third night of their stay, Clyde bought three Hershey bars to eat at bedtime while he read a book.

They had adjoining rooms. When Clyde went to bed, he turned on his heating pad, laid the Hershey bars down beside him and read until he fell asleep. When he awoke the next morning, the Hershey bars had melted all over the sheets.

When Chester called Clyde to meet him in the dining room for breakfast, Clyde said he would be right down.

The Disappearing Batteries

Noting the mess in the bed, Clyde called 'Digger O'Dell' at the front desk and told him Chester had been sick during the night and would he please send the cleaning women up to change Chester's bed. Clyde then quickly took the sheets off his bed and went to exchange them with Chester's sheets.

Clyde then joined Chester for breakfast. Chester thought that it took Clyde a long time to arrive but at the time didn't think much about it. After breakfast they passed by the front desk.

'Digger' told Chester, "I hope you feel much better now."

Chester turned to Clyde and asked, "What in the world is 'Digger' talking about?"

Clyde replied that he didn't know.

As they approached their rooms, the maids were just finishing up in Chester's room. The maids gave Chester a dirty look and said they hoped he was over the diarrhea and feeling better now.

It was not until later that Chester realized what Clyde had done.

Back on the case, they followed a company employee they had learned was a drug dealer to an apartment house. They noted the room he entered. Chester, standing on Clyde's shoulder, looked through the transom over the door of the apartment. He saw the employee in bed with a young woman.

They waited until he left and confronted him with cheating on his wife.

Pleading that his wife not be told of his infidelity, the employee became an informant in exchange for their silence about his 'affair.' He told them about one of his cohorts who stole batteries from the plant.

Returning to the plant, they quizzed the auditors about their inventory review to date. One day the auditors had calculated the inventory of batteries was 500 short and the next day inventory calculations showed 300 batteries over. The records were in such bad shape the auditors couldn't get a handle on the losses.

Based on information received from the informant, they hid in the parts and supplies warehouse the next night. Outside snow and ice covered the ground and the temperature was about zero. It was also very cold in the warehouse.

About 3:30 am in the morning a guard came through the warehouse. He was wearing a gun.

Chester turned to Clyde and said, "Wouldn't you know it. We'll be the only ones caught and probably shot by that idiot."

The guard passed by not seeing them hiding under a vehicle.

About 4:30 am, a big, black, muscular man entered through the outside warehouse door and crossed over to the battery storage area. He lifted three or four batteries in his arms and walked out the back door. This certainly showed us his strength.

In a few minutes he came back in and returned to the battery area.

Clyde turned to Chester and said, "Do you have a gun on you?"

Chester said, "Clyde, you know that I don't carry a gun."

Clyde said, "Then what are we going to do?"

Chester replied, "I guess when he goes outside the door, tackle him. You tackle him high and I'll tackle him low."

That is what they did.

The black man was more frightened then they were when tackled. Clyde ran his hands down the man's waist and legs searching for a weapon. The man was so shocked that he urinated all over himself and all over Clyde's hands.

The police were then called. Chester went to the police station where the police interviewed the employee.

During the interview, the policeman asked Chester, "How many batteries are you missing from the plant so far this year?"

This was about the end of February.

Not having received any accurate information from the auditors, Chester told the policeman, "249 batteries are missing."

The black man turned to Chester and said, "Hell, white boy, I done stole more than that this year myself."

The man was jailed and they began an extensive fraud and internal audit review at the plant that resulted in several of the company's employees being fired. Substantial dollar recoveries were made covering losses that had occurred.

After completing the review, it was time to head for home. In mid-winter in southeastern Wisconsin the weather was asserting itself in typical furious fashion with six-foot snow banks and a driving snowstorm confronting them as they headed for the O'Hare airport in Chicago.

The Disappearing Batteries

Running late as usual and trying to catch a 2:30 pm flight, Clyde, as the wheelman, barreled down the highway at 80 miles an hour in their rental car with an empty fuel tank and no open gas stations. The race was on; would they run out of gas before arriving in Chicago!

Arriving at O'Hare on gas fumes, they pulled up in front of the terminal with four whole minutes to spare before plane departure.

Clyde dashed from the car with the bags to the airline terminal counter to check in while Chester decided what to do with the rental car that was to be returned about a half mile away.

Just after Clyde jumped out of the car, a policeman knocked on the car window and told Chester that the car couldn't be parked there.

Chester told the policeman he needed to stop just a minute, as he had to run into the terminal to pick up a package. He asked the cop to please watch the car while he was gone as he would be back in a minute.

Chester left the car motor running and dashed out of the car to join Clyde as they ran for the departure gate. Everyone else was on board as they arrived. As soon as they boarded the airplane, it taxied away from the gate.

They speculated as to what the policeman did with the rental car.

Later that month when Chester received his rental car billing, there was no mention of any problem involving the return of the car.

KICKING BACK

Clyde and Chester were requested to go to a fruit and vegetable processing plant on the Texas/Mexico border to investigate continuing losses.

The plant imported vegetables and fruit from Mexico, packaged, and then shipped the produce to markets within the United States.

Obtaining imports from Mexico required contact and contracts with major Mexican growers and brokers. This was a highly competitive and risky business. Money management was essential.

The company had a very specific policy prohibiting cash advances to Mexican growers against future crop production and deliveries.

Upon arriving at the plant the first thing that Chester found in reviewing the books was that over $1,500,000 had been advanced to Mexican growers against their future crops. There was no collateral or means of guarantee of getting this money back.

Further investigation disclosed that most of the Mexican growers had taken the company's money and when their crops were harvested the products had been sold to other U.S. importers. Thus the money advanced was a total loss, although not yet written off on the plant books.

Further review of the client's books disclosed a strange entry of $75,000 that had been taken to other income the past month. No support of this entry was present. The credit entry that had originated from the West Coast division office was highly suspect.

Clyde called the company home office and related what had been found. They were advised to terminate the office employees, close down the office, and take all the books and records to the division office on the West Coast.

As they had gone to the plant in one of the company's airplanes, they dismissed the employees, packed up the records and Chester flew with them to the division office. Clyde returned home to pursue another matter.

Upon arriving and unloading the records at the division office, Chester went to the company's internal audit department to pursue the origin of the $75,000 entry.

Checking the cash receipt entries, Chester found that the $75,000 deposit had come from a check that had been issued by a box supplier company that the division had purchased substantial packaging supplies and materials.

Kicking Back

The check had been dated six months prior to the deposit. That meant someone had been holding the check for a considerable time. The check had nothing to do with the produce operation on the Mexican border.

It appeared that someone in the division office was using questionable kickbacks or rebates to offset losses in outlying plant operations.

Furthermore, a good possibility existed that this type of kickback or rebate was being received in violation of federal law.

Chester went to the division president's office and requested a meeting with him and the division executive vice president.

He advised them of his findings and suspicions. Chester further advised that what had been found might possibly be a federal offense and that if not immediately stopped and corrected might result in them going to jail.

The president immediately told Chester that this matter was none of his business and that he was going to call the company's home office and have Chester fired.

Chester picked up the telephone on the president's desk and started dialing.

The president asked, "What are you doing?"

Chester told him "You may not care if you go to jail, but I'm not going with you. I'm calling the chairman of the board in the home office to relate my findings and your resistance to a complete investigation of this matter."

The president told Chester, "Wait! Wait! Don't make that call. What do you want us to do?"

Chester told him he wanted the full story on how they got the checks, how many had been deposited against other plant operations, and how many checks were on hand that had not been deposited.

The executive vice president stated that he had a floor safe at his home that contained several checks that had not been deposited. He further stated that no other checks had been deposited other than the one Chester had found.

Chester went with the executive vice president to his home and the safe was opened. There were five checks totaling more than $400,000 in the safe. Obviously, these checks were being held until needed to cover up losses when occurred in outlying plant locations.

The checks were taken back to the division office. Chester advised that he was going to keep the checks and telephone the company's home office to send internal auditors to the division to examine the books to be sure no more checks had been deposited.

Furthermore, the auditors were going to be requested to audit the supplier company's books to determine if any other checks had been issued.

The checks Chester had confiscated were returned to the supplier companies. In addition, the $75,000 that had been deposited was reimbursed to the applicable supplier company.

Further, all of the divisions packaging suppliers were advised that the company did not require nor sanction rebates in order for them to do business with the company. Requirements for future packing materials were sent out for new bids and new purchase orders issued. Many of these companies advised that they were forbidden to bid in the past. This was probably because they wouldn't give kickbacks.

The president and executive vice president reluctantly agreed to this approach. Later they were severely reprimanded by the home office for their activities relating to this matter.

FALSE BANK DEPOSITS

Clyde and Chester were asked to go to a retail store in a southeastern state to investigate cash shortages.

They discovered that a loss had occurred as a result of the retail manager reporting fictitious deposits of daily receipts and pocketing the money.

Retail store procedures required the store manager or assistant store manager to complete a sales register report each morning and prepare for and deposit the previous day's receipts. Bank deposit slips were prepared in triplicate; the original retained by the bank, second copy transmitted to the retail store home office by mail the same day, and the third copy filed with the appropriate day's sales register report. The bank was requested to place a validation stamp on each copy of the deposit slip.

The company banking procedures dictated maintaining a $ 10,000 cash balance in the location account. Upon receipt of the second copy of the validated deposit slip, the home office would draw a draft on the bank for the amount of the deposit and placed such funds in a home office bank account.

They found that the store manager, over a period of time, had become friendly with the bank teller. As a result when he made a valid deposit, the manager, on some occasions, presented the second and third duplicate copies of a deposit slip with a prior day's date. He advised the bank teller that she had forgotten to validate such copies on a prior date when the deposit was made.

The store manager then had reflected on these fake copies of the bank deposits the amount of money taken in by the store on a prior date. The manager then pocketed that days cash receipts. However, The employee always sent the second copy to the home office. This procedure was duplicated several times during the two-week period until the manager had obtained $ 17,134.

Clyde and Chester had been asked to make a review at the store when the bank advised the home office that their account had been over drawn. The manager had disappeared by the time of their arrival.

The information they had obtained was turned over to the police. The manager was later arrested and charged with six counts of grand larceny. The former manager was tried, convicted, and sentenced to three years in prison.

The company used the findings of Clyde and Chester to initiate civil action against the bank. Banking connections were changed in the city. A statement had been obtained from the bank teller in which the teller admitted that she and the other tellers seldom look at the copies of the deposit slips to verify their accuracy—they just stamp and validate the duplicate copies. The tellers are so busy that only the original deposit slip is verified.

False Bank Deposits

The teller also acknowledged stamping on several occasions two duplicate copies of a deposit slip, which the company's employee claimed had inadvertently not been previously stamped by the teller.

The case went to trial and the company lost. The court held that the original copy of the deposit sip was the only legal instrument in the transaction for which the bank could incur any liability.

OUT OF TRUST

After completing an investigation into stolen parts from the company's farm equipment production parts storage area, Clyde and Chester were requested to investigate a substantial loss due to sales of equipment out-of-trust.

A sale out-of-trust occurs when a dealer finances the floor planning of a new piece of equipment and then upon sale of that equipment changes the paper work to reflect that another piece of equipment was the one financed and retained the money from the sale for his own use. Thus the company has in effect financed the same piece of equipment twice.

The company had experienced about $12,000,000 in losses due to dealer agricultural equipment sales out-of-trust.

They learned that one former dealer, responsible for a substantial portion of the company loss, was seen in the area of a small town in southern Wisconsin. Even though over 30 inches of snow was on the ground, they believed their rental car could be driven to the area where the dealer was spotted.

On the way to that location, they spotted two new pieces of the company's equipment parked beside a farmer's barn.

They pulled into the barn area and checked the serial numbers on the equipment. The equipment was not on the list of double financed equipment. They went to the back porch of the farmer's house and knocked on the door.

A little old lady came to the door and they questioned her about any knowledge she had about the former dealer. She didn't want to talk but they persisted.

As it was about zero degrees outside with a driving snow, Chester asked if they could come inside to talk, as he was about to freeze. The lady hesitated but finally asked them to come inside the porch area.

They sat down and continued their discussion about the dealer. It was dark on the porch. The lady was sitting about ten feet away and working on something in her lap. As his eyes became adjusted to the darkness, Chester saw two eyes shining from a tub in her lap. He soon noticed the most awful smell coming from that area.

Chester asked, " What in the world are you doing?"

The lady replied that she was scraping the meat off of a hog's head with her fingernails to make hog's head cheese.

As Chester was about to throw up from the sight and smell, he and Clyde got up and went outside.

They did learn that the former dealer had just been to her house about a piece of used equipment she had bought and was on his way to Madison, Wisconsin to catch an airplane for Chicago and then subsequently on to Florida.

Clyde said, "Come on, we can catch up with him at the airport."

Off they went at about 100 miles an hour in the driving snow with eight foot snow drifts at the side of the road on their way to Madison about 45 miles away. Clyde drove, as he said he had been a wheelman in the CID.

Chester figured that this was the end of the line for them on that slick highway.

The heavens smiled on them and they arrived safely in Madison only to learn that the airplane had just left for Chicago with their man on board.

Chester found a charter pilot and made arrangements for him to fly them to Chicago. Following the charter pilot, they boarded a small single engine airplane and departed into the fog and snow.

As they were flying only slightly above the light poles and telephone lines, Chester asked, "Why are you flying so low?"

The pilot replied that there wasn't much gasoline in the plane but thought that they could make it into O'Hare.

Chester asked "Why didn't you buy gas before we left?"

The pilot replied, "I didn't have any money to buy gas!"

Chester said, "All you had to do was ask, we would have advanced the money."

At about that time the airplane radio started to go out. It would work for about two minutes and then go off for about two minutes.

Clyde asked, "What's wrong with the radio?"

The pilot replied, "Don't worry, it doesn't work half the time."

Chester then asked, "How in the world are we going to get landing instructions at O'Hare if the radio goes out?"

The pilot replied, "I can find O'Hare all right but we are going to have to land soon as we are about out of gas."

Approaching O'Hare with the radio out and no contact with the control tower, the sky was full of big jets taking off and landing. The small plane was almost hit several times.

The pilot headed right for an active runway and started down.

Chester turned to Clyde and said, "The airport security are going to be all over us once we land. Grab your bag and as soon as this guy stops you and I are going to make a run for the terminal."

Sure enough, after dodging several jets, the little airplane set down on the runway and Chester could see about six security vehicles heading for the plane.

Just as the plane stopped on the runway it was surrounded by security. Chester threw the agreed upon amount of money at the pilot and he and Clyde jumped out of the airplane and ran towards the terminal.

As luck would have it, Frank Sinatra's private jet was parked next to the terminal and surrounded by a lot of spectators. They ran for Sinatra's jet and disappeared into the crowd. Looking back, they could see the pilot being placed in a security car and driven away.

Checking into the Miami departure area in the terminal, they learned that the former dealer had just left on an airplane bound for Miami.

Again, they were about five minutes too late. But after this frightening experience, they felt that their luck had just about run out so they departed for home to check on the out-of-trust losses another day.

CREDIT AND COLLECTIONS

The home office noticed that one of its retail stores had open past-due accounts amounting to over $ 1,000,000. Pressure was asserted on store personnel to improve collection efforts.

When collection of past-due accounts did not improve, Clyde and Chester were asked to review the retail store operations.

During the review they found that a collection agency had been engaged to collect past-due receivables on a 25% fee basis. It was later discovered that the store credit manager was a close friend of certain collection agency personnel.

The store credit manager selected various accounts that, after the store controller's approval, were turned over to the credit agency. The company credit manager maintained no collection effort records. In addition, no log was maintained on accounts turned over to the collection agency.

To refer an account to the collection agency, the credit manager merely photocopied the accounts receivable card and either had it delivered or sent the photocopy to the agency without a cover letter. Upon receipt of the photocopy, the agency was authorized to begin collection efforts.

Two months before Clyde and Chester's arrival, the store controller had been discharged for falsifying receipts of over $ 200 to cover petty cash shortages.

They determined that the store controller authorized "adjusted fee payments" to the collection agency in the amount of $ 4,400 for three accounts that were not collected. The three accounts involved an insurance claim, a bad debt write-off, and a reverse entry. This fraud was discovered when the current statement from the collection agency was reviewed. It was also discovered that several current accounts had been turned over to the agency, accounts that the credit manager could have easily collected.

A $ 100,000 receivable from a major oil company that was a little over thirty days due was turned over to the agency. The account had been collected and the agency retained a $ 25,000 fee.

In a period of about two months the agency had received $45,000 in fees.

Clyde and Chester terminated the agency's services as well as the credit manager. A recovery of $ 40,000 was made from the collection agency reducing the company's actual loss from $ 85,000 to $ 45,000.

Further review disclosed that the credit manager had been terminated by his former employer due to a shortage in his accounts that had been turned over to the bonding company. This meant that the remaining company loss could not be recovered under its fidelity bond. The employee was not insurable since a prior bond claim had established his fraudulent activities.

The company attorney's recommended against pursuing criminal action against the credit agency. The store apparently did not want any bad publicity that might be made public.

Later, the former credit manager was investigated by the FBI for fraud against his subsequent employer and arrested.

CONVERSION OF CUSTOMER'S PAYMENTS

When the new retail manager of a small agriculture equipment store assumed his duties after the former manager resigned, one of his first endeavors was to review the accounts receivable aging.

The new manager noticed a substantial overdue balance outstanding from the sale of a used machine. The new manager had the equipment repossessed.

The customer came to the store and threatened to sue the company as he stated payments were current. The customer stated that he had given the former store manager cash on three or more occasions that totaled $9,000.

The customer further stated that on two occasions the former manager went to the bank with him to cash checks issued to the customer by a contracting firm in the amount of about $3,000 each.

In each case, the customer gave the former store manager about $2,300 in cash.

Further review established that the former retail store manager was in fact present with the customer at the bank when the customer's checks were cashed.

The piece of equipment was then returned to the customer.

The new store manager requested that Clyde and Chester conduct an investigation to determine if there were other instances of conversion of company funds by the former store manager.

Upon arrival at the city where the store was located, they visited with the store's customer who had brought the matter to the attention of the new retail store manager. They advised the customer that they felt he was truthful in his explanations. However, it was suggested that he take a polygraph examination, as this would assist the police when they were called into the matter.

The customer agreed to take a polygraph examination and passed.

Further investigation by them disclosed that the former retail store manager sold several items of used equipment at big discounts to himself under guise of a fictitious company. He later sold the equipment at an auction that netted $40,000 that was converted to his own use.

In addition, the former manager was found to have traded used equipment he owned in a fictitious company for new equipment. The used equipment was overvalued by about $15,000.

Conversion Of Customer's Payments

The information obtained during the investigation was turned over to the police.

The former manager was arrested based on a complaint filed by the customer from whom the former retail store manager took $9,000 in cash.

A fidelity insurance bond filed covering the $64,000 loss was collected. Additionally, a civil suit was initiated against the former manager to recover the $64,000 loss.

Recoveries from the civil suits were remitted to the bonding company as it had already paid the company for the loss.

BANKING

THE VOID CERTIFICATES OF DEPOSIT

Clyde and Chester were called to a CEO's office and told he was concerned about the company's major investment in a local bank.

Nothing specific was known other than the president and vice-president of the bank recently appeared to begin living considerably beyond their income.

Chester went out to the bank to make a cursory review. The outside auditors were at the bank making their annual review. The auditors had been there several weeks. In addition, the federal bank examiners had been there for six weeks. Chester felt that if there was anything obvious in the books the auditors should have already found such irregularities.

Chester called the CEO and said that if the bank examiners and public auditors hadn't found any irregularity yet there seemed to be no problem. Chester was told to stay at the bank until he found something.

Chester went back to the bank and tried to think of areas the auditors might not have considered. Chester sat in a chair at the back of the bank and thought of what he would do if he defrauded the bank. Chester thought that the area of Certificates of Deposit would be an area where significant money could be stolen. He observed the employees at work for a while and noticed that the vice president and cashier seemed to be overly friendly. Chester then asked to see the Certificate of Deposit Book.

In browsing through that book he noted an unusual amount of "void" Certificates of Deposit. The numbered stubs in the book were marked void.

Chester found this to be unusual, as the voided certificates would normally be either left attached or scotch taped to the stubs.

Chester called Clyde and advised him that he was suspicious that bank employees were showing Certificate of Deposits as void, but then later certain bank employees filled them out to pledge at another bank as collateral for personal loans. This would leave the bank responsible for any losses if the borrower defaulted in payment of the loans.

Chester asked Clyde to call the CEO and advise him of his suspicions. Chester also asked Clyde to request the CEO to use his resources at three of the major local banks to determine if any of the bank Certificates of Deposit had been pledged for loans, particularly by any of the bank employees.

A few days later the CEO called Clyde and said, "Guess what? We have more than $4,000,000 in CD's pledged as collateral at two local banks for loans to my president and vice president."

The Void Certificates Of Deposit

Clyde and Chester were told to go to the bank and find out who was involved.

They went to the bank. As they felt another employee was involved with the other two, they began interviewing all employees. They soon found that one of the women who handled the Certificates of Deposit register was having an affair with the vice president.

Clyde called the woman in for an interview. She soon admitted to helping her boss dummy the CD register but denied getting any money or any monetary benefit from her activities.

Clyde then called in the bank president. After extensive interrogation, the president admitted that he and the vice president were using the 'voided' Certificates of Deposit as collateral for loans at two local banks.

The officers had set up a private company to trade commodities planning to make a lot of money. They thought that the loans could then be repaid and recover the CD's that were collateralized.

Their luck ran out and they experienced a series of major losses. They continued borrowing against more of the fraudulent Certificates of Deposits in hope of earning enough money to cover additional losses realized by expanding their activities into trading options and real estate. In reality, they lost most of the money they had obtained.

Clyde obtained statements from the president and vice president outlining their fraudulent actions. They were turned over to the police for prosecution.

Chester filed a fidelity bond insurance claim for the bank in order to recover the $4,000,000 in bank loss from the fraud.

THE PHONY BANK LOANS

The Chairman of the Board of a local bank requested Clyde and Chester to investigate loans made by one of his black loan officers. Several loans, which initially looked proper, were beginning to look questionable.

Clyde always had a policy that once you start interrogating people and began taking statements, all investigative leads are pursued even if fraud leads all the way to the top man.

Accordingly, Clyde asked the Chairman if he had anything to hide. If so, he might not want to start an investigation that might also lead to him.

The Chairman told Clyde that he was clean and had nothing to hide.

Clyde said, "Fine, Chester and I will start the investigation." However, Clyde told the banker that the investigative findings would be reported directly to the board of directors. The banker agreed with this approach.

Chester went to the bank to begin reviewing loan files originated by the suspect loan officer.

The Federal Bank Examiners had been at the bank for the past few weeks and had most of the loan files in the boardroom. So far, the examiners had found no improprieties.

Chester entered the boardroom and asked for the loan files containing the six largest loans made by the black loan officer.

When they gave Chester the files they asked, "What are you going to do with them?"

Chester said, "I'm going to hit the street to interview each of the makers of these notes to be sure everything is in order."

The bank examiners told Chester, "You can't do that!"

Chester told them, "You just watch me!"

Chester looked at the files and arranged them in the order he planned the interviews.

The first file covered loans to a black junk and scrap dealer. The initial loan made three years ago had been for $ 3,000. The current loan balance outstanding was over $ 100,000. All the notes seemed to have been appropriately signed by the maker.

The Phony Bank Loans

However, it seemed strange that each time the loan was renewed, the loan balance had been increased by several thousand dollars. The difference in loan balances, less accrued interest, was paid by issuance of a cashiers check payable to the maker of the note rather than the proceeds being credited to the maker's bank account. This procedure appeared unusual.

Chester drove to the junkyard and found the owner in his office. Chester showed the owner the note covering the first loan and asked if the signature was his.

He said that it was. Chester asked if his business dealings with the bank had been satisfactory. Again, he said the bank had been very helpful.

Making a stab in the dark, Chester asked the junk dealer if it was true that when each note became due the loan officer came to his office and asked him to sign a new note in blank.

The dealer said, "Yes that was what the loan officer had done. That saved me going to the bank. As far as I know the new loan was always made out in the amount of the old loan balance plus the accrued interest."

The junk dealer was then asked if he knew what his current loan balance was at the bank. He replied that the balance was about $ 6,000. Chester asked if he would be surprised to know that the bank records showed that he owed over $100,000.

The junk dealer said, "No way!" He then got belligerent and told Chester to leave.

Chester advised the junk dealer that he could either talk to him now or he could go down town and talk to the District Attorney.

Further, Chester told him he didn't know whether he had conspired with the loan officer or if the officer had acted alone to defraud the bank. If he wanted to risk going to jail that was fine with Chester.

The junk dealer said, "There's no way I'm going to get involved with the District Attorney's office. I don't know anything about these bank loans other than I know I don't owe $ 100,000. What do you want with me?"

Chester told the junk dealer that he just wanted the truth. Chester told him what he thought had happened.

He told the dealer he believed that after the junk dealer signed the notes in blank the loan officer took the notes back to the bank and filled in amounts substantially higher than the amount owed.

Chester believed that the loan officer had a deal with someone else in the bank to cut a cashiers check for the excess, then cash the cashiers check at the bank, and pocket the money.

Chester showed all the notes to the junk dealer. He said that what Chester had told him must be true, as he never got any more money from the bank than the original $3,000. Furthermore, he had no knowledge of the face value of the notes being increased each time.

Chester took a detailed signed statement from the junk dealer. Chester telephoned Clyde and informed him of the content of the statement.

Clyde telephoned the Chairman at the bank and requested a meeting of the Board of Directors that night.

At the meeting of the board, Clyde presented Chester's findings to date and said it appeared that most of the loans processed by the loan officer had been handled the same way as covered in the statement Chester had taken from the junk dealer. The board was asked if the bank carried Fidelity Bond Insurance.

The board was told that if they had such insurance, the investigation would be conducted with the objective of recovering through insurance the bank's losses due to the officer's fraudulent activities. They were told that the bank carried such insurance.

Clyde advised the board that the next steps to be taken, if they agreed, would be for Clyde to begin interrogating the loan officer in question while Chester reviewed all loans made by the officer to determine the potential loss.

The board instructed that if the findings to date proved correct, they should also proceed to seek prosecution of the loan officer.

The next day, Clyde called the loan officer into an office at the bank and confronted him with the junk dealer's signed statement and several of the related cashiers checks.

The loan officer finally admitted that he had obtained signatures on blank notes and had later filled them out with amounts considerably higher than the original legitimate loan.

Cashiers checks issued for the difference had been prepared by his girl friend that worked as cashier in the bank. She cashed the checks and gave him the money. Signed statements were obtained from the loan officer and the cashier. The loan officer admitted having diverted over $1,000,000 to his own use.

However, in the course of the interrogation, the loan officer also stated that the chairman of the board had his own deal to convert money to his own use.

The Phony Bank Loans

The loan officer related that the bank had several thousand shares of common stock outstanding in public hands. There generally was no market for the stock. The original issue price had been about $ 20.

When a stockholder wanted to sell his stock, he called the Chairman of the Board who made the only market in the stock. The banker usually told the stockholder that there was presently very little market for the stock. He would try his best although he might not get more than $ 10 a share. If the stockholder agreed, the banker then sought a buyer at $ 18 to $ 20 a share.

He paid the selling stockholder $ 10 a share and pocketed the difference. This information had also been incorporated into the loan officer's signed statement.

A board meeting was called again and the loan officer's signed statement was presented and discussed.

Clyde and Chester were told the loan officer and cashier would be terminated and to turn the information over to the district attorney for prosecution. Chester was instructed to file a fidelity bond insurance claim to recover the loss.

Clyde presented the information the loan officer had given about the Chairman's stock dealings. The board asked the Chairman if that information was true.

The Chairman reluctantly admitted that it was true. The board immediately voted to fire the Chairman.

The loan officer was successfully prosecuted and the bank's loss recovered from a fidelity bond insurance claim prepared by Chester.

The Chairman lost his job because he didn't think it possible that he would get caught up in the investigation. Later, the Chairman's wife telephoned Chester and cussed him out for her husband losing his job when he had hired them in the first place. She was advised that her husband had been warned initially that if he had any involvement he should not hire us.

HIDDEN ASSETS

A banking client called Chester to review a bank loan that been in default for almost ten years. The bank had written off the loan. A judgment had been filed against the maker of the $500,000 loan when the loan became due and was not paid.

As the judgment had been in effect for almost ten years, the bank had to make a decision whether or not to go to the trouble and expense to renew the judgment for another ten years.

Obviously, the bank did not want to renew the judgment unless there was some possibility of future collection. The bank asked Chester to review the loan file and do a background check on the person who had made the loan to determine if there were hidden assets that might be pursued to satisfy the debt.

Chester reviewed the loan file documents and the loan agreement. The financial statement submitted by the loan applicant was a joint financial statement covering the assets of the maker and his wife. Substantial assets had been reported including a home in one of the finest neighborhoods in the city.

However, when these assets were pursued when the loan went into default, the bank discovered that title to all of the assets listed on the financial statement were all in the name of the wife. Since the loan was made and signed only by the husband, the wife's separate assets could not be attached.

Beginning his review, Chester drove by the couple's residence and noted its value at about $900,000. New Lincoln and Cadillac automobiles were in the driveway.

A review of the local courthouse records disclosed that title to the house was still in the wife's name. A check with auto registrations showed that title to the cars was also in the wife's name. No other assets were located in the county.

Obviously, due to the life style the man and his wife were enjoying, substantial income must be originating from some hidden source.

In order to possibly obtain some financial information on the individual, Chester picked up the trash at the residence over the next three weeks.

Going through all of the garbage in trash bags is a very disgusting and sickening experience. You cannot imagine what you find. However, Chester found some interesting information. Copies of duplicate bank deposit slips and bank envelopes lead to several bank accounts. Unfortunately, each of the bank accounts was in the wife's name only.

Hidden Assets

Check stubs from an oil royalty check was found. The stub identified royalties from oil and gas wells located in several distant counties. The stubs indicated that royalty income totaled over $25,000 a month.

Chester drove to all of the counties identified by the royalty stubs and reviewed courthouse records searching for recorded mineral rights and assignments. In checking through the records, several properties were identified where the maker of the bank note had inherited mineral rights from his father's estate.

In each case, the mineral interest was recorded solely in the name of the maker of the bank loan. This meant that the bank could use the judgment to pursue the mineral rights and royalty income.

The individual had successfully hidden these assets for almost ten years and probably felt comfortable that they would never be found and attached.

Chester reported his findings to the bank. The bank promptly renewed the judgment against the individual.

The judgment was then successfully filed to attach the mineral interest and royalty income.

When the judgment liens had been recorded, the individual was notified of the bank's action. When the individual learned that the hidden assets and income had been attached, he quickly scheduled a meeting with the bank. He shortly arranged for full payment of the past due note plus accrued interest.

BILKING THE BANK

When certain possible irregularities appeared during a routine review by a federal bank examiner, the president of a local bank called in Clyde and Chester to conduct an investigation. During their review the following scenario unfolded.

Certain officers and a director of the bank had begun investing in the stock market. Investments were made in the trade names of companies that actually were partnership ventures of the individuals.

Improper loans were made to these trade name companies over a two-year period until the partnerships had suffered a $250,000 loss in the stock market through investments in highly speculative stocks.

Additional loans were made to pay the interest on the old loans until the debt escalated to $325,000.

The bank officer's set up new trade name companies to invest in real estate in an attempt to make back money in order to reduce the debt of the other partnerships.

As the real estate investments increased and also failed to produce profits, the old notes had to be retired. The employees then converted funds from certain customer accounts to retire the old loans.

Additional funds were converted in this manner from customer accounts and through fraudulent loans made to fictitious companies and partnerships until $750,000 had been obtained. Over $200,000 of this money was transferred to one of the employee's personal bank accounts in another city.

The bank maintained account balances at a correspondent bank.

The employees in several different ways obtained money for investment and personal use. In some instances, one of the employees telephoned the correspondent bank requesting the bank's account be charged and those funds wire transferred to another bank's account for credit to still another bank's account in another city for deposit into the account of the employee making the telephone call.

When the bank received the correspondent bank's statement at month-end, the employee's name on the bank wire transfer ticket was erased and a fictitious name inserted in order that the bank files would not disclose the fraudulent transfer. The entry at the bank was made against various customers' accounts.

Fictitious savings accounts were also established at the bank to which customer funds were transferred. Subsequently, cashier's checks were purchased payable to a fictitious name and charged against the savings account. Each cashier's check was used

Bilking The Bank

to purchase another cashier's check payable to another fictitious name. This check was then used to purchase a cashier's check payable to the bank employee who then transmitted the check for deposit to his bank account in another city.

In addition, one of the employees took several of the bank's blank Certificate of Deposit forms and marked the control book void for the pre-numbered certificates.

The employee then typed in appropriate information indicating that he was the owner of the certificate with a face value of a certain amount. The employee then took the CD's to another bank where he pledged them as collateral for personal loans.

The bank's accounts were audited each year by public accountants and audited twice a year by the federal bank examiners.

However, discovery of the fraud was not made until about two years into the fraudulent activities.

The bank officers successfully concealed from the public accountants shortages in customer accounts and fictitious loans. Fictitious loans were made in the names of companies or partnerships for which the employees had rented post office boxes in the area.

When the auditors mailed note confirmations, the employees received them at the post office box and signed them under their assumed names as being correct and returned them to the bank.

Shortages in customer accounts were concealed from the customers through pulling out the computer-printed bank statement at the end of each month. A bank statement was typed each month for the customer leaving out the unauthorized entries and changing the daily balance so that the typed copy sent to the customer agreed with or reconciled to the records of the customer.

On one occasion, the auditors got the actual balances from the computer and sent customers account confirmations based on such balances.

As the bank employees knew which customers' accounts were short, they telephoned these customers to bring their account confirmations to the bank whereupon they explained that a new computer system had been initiated that had messed up all customer account activity. Each customer was given a newly typed bank statement showing the account balances, as they should have been.

The customers were asked to sign the audit confirmations, even though the balances on the confirmations were erroneous, in order to expedite the audit and allow the bank time to correct the computer system.

Clyde and Chester presented the bank with their findings. The bank immediately terminated the employees and called in the FBI to initiate an investigation towards prosecution of the former employees.

Chester subsequently prepared, filed, and collected a fidelity bond insurance claim to recover the bank's $750,000 loss.

The former bank employees were prosecuted.

USING THE BANK AS A FICTITIOUS PAYEE

A Mid-Western company acquired a local company. As sometimes occurs, the vice-president and the controller felt that after the company was acquired they would be without jobs.

The controller of the acquired corporation had authority to approve invoices, cause checks to be issued, and sign company checks.

The controller, during an eleven-month period preceding completion of the acquisition, caused eleven checks to be drawn payable to his bank in amounts totaling $204,000 and made payable from an operating account maintained in the same bank. The vice-president and controller of the company signed these checks.

As it is common practice for many corporations to draw checks payable to its bank for employee/employer social security deposits, employee withholding tax deposits, income tax quarterly deposits, and other matters, bank tellers handle many checks prepared in this fashion.

The controller maintained two personal bank accounts at the same bank; one carried as a special account and the other in the name of a personally owned company.

In several instances, either the vice-president or controller would take one of these checks to the bank and present it for deposit.

When these checks drawn payable to the U.S. Treasury were presented to the bank for deposit, bank deposit slips were given to the teller covering deposit of the checks into either the controller's special account or the account of his personal company.

The bank teller rubber-stamped an endorsement on the back of the check showing "For Deposit Only to the name of the Bank." In one instance, the controller signed his name on the back of the check.

Soon after the acquisition of the corporation was complete, the new owner discovered this and other frauds, filed bond claims, and initiated appropriate criminal actions.

The bonding company paid the claims and then sought recovery of the $204,000 loss on the checks from its insured's bank through civil action.

The bank engaged Clyde and Chester to review the matter and advise it on a course of action to take.

After reviewing the facts, they suggested that the bank file a bond claim of $224,000 against the fidelity insurance carrier under its Banker's Blanket Bond for any

Using The Bank As A Fictitious Payee

loss the bank might incur from this matter including provision for $20,000 in legal costs. They also suggested that the bank demand the bonding company assume its timely defense of such legal action.

In this instance, it was quite clear that the bank customers' officers had never intended that the bank receive any of the proceeds from the checks or have an interest in the money in any way. Such checks were merely used as a devise to extract money from the individuals' employer.

The bank's claim was filed under those sections of the insurance agreement relating to on-premises loss of property through common-law or statutory larceny and false pretenses and under that portion of the forgery and alteration section relating to any check or draft made payable to a fictitious payee and endorsed in the name of such fictitious payee which shall be deemed to be forged as to such endorsement.

As they had advised, the bank's position prevailed; no loss was incurred and the bank's bonding company did not have to assume liability.

TRUSTING THE TRUST OFFICER

A company owned a substantial interest in a local bank. The bank had a large trust department managed by several personnel and supervised by a trust department vice president.

The trust department managed customer funds deposited in trust with the bank for investment, collection of income, and subsequent distribution of income and principle to designated persons in accordance with the various customer trust instruments executed with the bank.

When a senior bank officer noticed that the trust vice president seemed to be living somewhat beyond his means, he called Clyde and Chester to review the trust department operations.

The trust vice president had been with the bank 17 years and was well liked by his associates and trust department customers.

A background check confirmed that the trust officer was in fact living beyond his income at the bank. Further background checks and interviews confirmed that the trust officer had begun investing in speculative stocks during the past year.

Chester reviewed activity in one of the largest trust funds that revealed some unusual transactions. Tracing these transactions through the books disclosed that the trust officer was diverting funds to his own personal use.

Clyde called the trust officer into a bank conference room and began interrogating him about the diversion of trust funds.

The trust officer finally admitted that handling so much money for others made him greedy for the better life. He had just "borrowed" money from one of the trusts to invest in the stock market hoping to hit it big. Then he would repay the money to the trust.

As luck would have it, everything he invested was lost.

He had diverted about $ 400,000 by the time he was caught. Not all the money had gone towards stock purchases. He had bought his wife a fur coat and a new car. He also spent lavishly on entertainment.

The trust officer had very little to offer towards restitution. After Clyde obtained a signed statement of confession, the trust officer was terminated.

Chester immediately helped the trust officer gather up all his personal belongings and then took him home.

Trusting The Trust Officer

Once a bank employee is caught in fraud, he is out of the banking business for life, as he is no longer bondable.

A complete audit of all the trust accounts was made to verify that all the losses had been uncovered.

They advised the bank president of the results of the review and suggested that the he call the principals of the trust to the bank and advise them of the situation. The bank president said he was afraid that they would pull their substantial deposits out of the bank. He said he just couldn't talk to them about the event and would Clyde talk to them and assure them they had incurred no loss.

Clyde called the individuals and asked them to come to his office. This couple was very wealthy having inherited several hundred million dollars.

Clyde sent a car and driver to pick them up. They were told about their accounts being invaded by the bank trust employee but that after an internal audit determined the shortage, their account was restored in full. In addition, the bank's public accounting firm will perform an audit of their account. They were in a hurry and didn't seem concerned. She was in a hurry to get to a hair appointment. Clyde told them they had the car for the day. He also made reservations at the bank's expense for them to have dinner at the top tony restaurant in town. Based on their wealth, they seemed to have no concern about what was a minor occurrence to them.

The bank president was very pleased with the outcome.

A fidelity bond insurance claim covering the bank's loss was filed in the amount of $400,000 and subsequently collected.

The bank chose not to prosecute the Trust officer, as they did not want to incur the publicity of a trial.

TAKING A STATEMENT

One of the things an investigator always has to keep in mind is to dot all the "I's" and cross all the "T's" when taking a statement of confession. If the statements were used in a court trial, they had to survive defendant lawyer's cross-examination.

This case, even though it involves a very small amount of money, shows what can happen if the investigation is not conducted or a statement not taken in the proper way.

The company received millions of dollars in the mail each day as well as thousands of other letters. In addition, a vast amount of mail was sent within the company offices between various departments.

A central mail room was responsible for receiving and distributing all incoming mail as well as preparing all outgoing mail for pick up by the post office.

With this large number of pieces of mail being handled, there is always the possibility for attempted fraud.

The mailroom employed several young men and women to distribute mail to the various departments within the company.

A central treasury department was the recipient of all incoming checks that were delivered to the department by mailroom personnel.

In addition, sometime checks were sent from other departments to the treasury department. Company policy dictated that no cash was to be sent through interoffice mail.

However, on this one occasion, a person in one department sent several checks and a one hundred dollar bill by interoffice mail to the treasury department with a cover statement listing the amounts transmitted.

When the envelope was received in the treasury department, it was short by the one hundred dollar bill.

Company treasury department personnel requested Chester to investigate.

Chester reviewed the contents of the envelope and questioned the employee receiving the transmittal. The employee remembered that a young black man about 20 years old had made the mail run that contained the envelope in question.

Chester contacted the transmitter of the envelope and was assured that the envelope did contain the one hundred dollar bill.

Chester reviewed the matter with Clyde. The amount of the loss was not that significant but it could be indicative of some larger scheme that may exist or was just beginning.

The young man who delivered the mail to the treasury department was summoned to Clyde's office and questioned about the missing money.

He continuously denied taking the money. Clyde asked him if he had any objections to taking a polygraph exam. The young man agreed to take a polygraph exam and Chester, with another of the company's employees, took the young man to the polygraph examiners office.

The examiner, after the first test, told Chester the young man was not telling the truth but at that point he didn't know whether he had taken the money or had knowledge of someone else taking the money.

Chester suggested the questions be more specific to determine if money on a larger scale was being taken by anyone in the mail department.

After the second test, the examiner told Chester the young man was again failing the test. The examiner felt that the young man had taken the money and that he had no knowledge of anyone else participating in a similar scheme.

Chester asked the examiner to give one more test. The results of the third test still showed the young man had an involvement in the missing one hundred dollar bill.

Chester went into the examination room with the examiner to talk with the young man. Chester went over the problem at hand covering the delivery of the mail and the disappearance of the money that could only have been done by the young man.

Chester had a pad of paper and pen and told the young man he was going to take a statement from him as to what had happened.

As Chester started to write, the young man said he would tell him what he had done but that he wasn't going to sign any statement.

Chester told him that was fine. He said, "I just want to write down for the record exactly what happened."

Chester wrote out in longhand a statement that contained words similar to the following:

> On this date, Mr. XYZ has given the following oral statement. Company A employs me in the mailroom and it is my responsibility to deliver mail from the mailroom to all the departments located in the building. Today, (month,

> day year), I picked up mail from the production department and delivered it to the treasury department. One of the envelopes contained several checks and a one hundred dollar bill. I admit to taking the one hundred dollar bill from the envelope and putting it in my pocket. It is my desire now to give the one hundred dollar bill to Chester for his return to the treasury department.

At this point Chester read back what he had written down and asked the young man if what he had written was true and correct?

The young man said, "That is correct."

Chester then added to the statement the following:

> I, Chester Karrick, have written this statement on this date (M,D,YR) based on information given to me orally by Mr. XYZ, who admits that this statement is true and correct but has refused to sign it.

Chester then signed the bottom of the statement. He then turned to the polygraph examiner and asked him if he had heard Chester read the statement and the young man say that the content was true and correct.

The polygraph examiner said that he had heard the young man's oral admission to taking the money.

Chester asked him to sign on the statement under an additional comment Chester added which said, "I witnessed the above statement being read to Mr. XYZ and he admitted to me that it is true and correct."

Chester then called the employee from the company and an employee of the polygraph company into the room.

Again Chester read the statement he had written and asked the young man if it was true and correct. Again, he said that it was true.

Chester asked the other two to sign their names on the bottom of the statement.

Chester was aware that an oral admission witnessed by others was as good as a signed statement by the accused.

Chester then told the young man that he was terminated from the company and he would accompany him back to the company to get his personal belongings.

Taking A Statement

As it was then about 6:00 pm in the evening, the young man asked Chester if he would also take him to the downtown college where he was due in class that night.

They picked up the personal belongings at the company and Chester took him to school.

The next morning at about 9:00 am, Chester got a call from Clyde to come to his office immediately as there was trouble over the prior evenings investigation.

Arriving in Clyde's office, Clyde told Chester that he had just received a telephone call from an ACLU lawyer who said that his client was wrongly accused of theft and his employment wrongly terminated.

The lawyer told Clyde, "I am going to sue you, Chester, and the company for all they are worth."

Chester showed Clyde the statement taken the past evening and that he had left the young man at college. It was obvious that the young man had gone home to his mother and lied about not having stolen money. The mother in turn had called the lawyer.

Clyde read the statement and quickly grabbed the phone and called the lawyer.

Clyde told the lawyer, "Listen, while I read to you the statement Chester prepared and had witnessed by several individuals."

When Clyde finished reading the statement, the lawyer said, "Aw hell, the kid lied to his mother; forget the whole thing."

The lesson here is that even though you can't always get a signed confession from the perpetrator, you can successfully accomplish your mission by using your head and getting appropriate witnesses to your interview and oral admissions. Chester had been especially careful since he was dealing with a young minority.

AUTOMOTIVE PARTS AND EQUIPMENT

HORSE BARNS AND FENCES

Clyde and Chester were requested to make a security review at a mid-western state plant that manufactured automotive jacks.

They usually scheduled arrival at a location on the day before the planned review. This allowed time for driving around the city to observe where plant management lived in order to get a feel for their standard of living.

While driving by the plant maintenance manager's house, they noted that he lived on about five acres of land bordered by a new wood fence. A big new wood barn was also on the property.

Chester speculated that the lumber used for the fence and barn had been charged to the plant.

After a late dinner that evening, they drove by the plant to observe the late shift worker's activity as the plant operated twenty-four hours a day. The plant was well lighted but from the outside no activity inside the plant was evident.

They entered the plant unobserved by a guard. The guards were not at their assigned locations. They observed that no workers were present in the production area although all the lights were on.

Noticing stairs that led to an upstairs floor, Chester proceeded up to an area completely dark. Finding a light switch just inside a door, he flipped the switch and he was almost trampled. About twenty-five employees stormed by him rushing downstairs.

Over thirty cots were counted in the big room upstairs. Apparently the late shift workers showed up to work on time and then left the work area about 9:30 pm to go upstairs to sleep the rest of the night.

There was no telling how long this system had gone unobserved. It was obvious plant management never checked on the night shift or on their lack of product production.

Upon arriving at the plant the next day, the plant manager was asked to take them on a review of the maintenance area. Chester wanted to know what lumber materials were used in the plant.

While walking through the maintenance area they noted that the only lumber being used in the maintenance shop was 1 x 2 wood. They were told that this lumber was used to build pallets for storage and shipment of plant products.

The plant manager was then requested to pull all purchase orders and paid invoices relating to lumber purchases made by the plant during the past two years.

A review of the documents showed that the maintenance manager had initiated the purchase of substantial amounts of 4 x 4, 2 x 4, 1 x 4, 1 x 6 and other lumber materials and supplies. The maintenance manager authorized the issuance of each purchase order. He had also signed the receiving reports and approved the invoices for payment.

The plant manager acknowledged that none of this lumber had been required nor used by the plant.

The maintenance manager was called into the office. Clyde interrogated him about the lumber purchases.

In the statement taken by Clyde, the man readily admitted using the lumber for his own personal use to build his barn and fences and charging the $40,000 cost to plant maintenance.

The man was terminated and turned over to the authorities for prosecution.

Although they were at the plant only to perform a perimeter security review, it became evident that considerable theft was taking place at the plant location. While walking through the maintenance area Clyde stopped by a lathe operator and asked him, "Which door is it that the employees are carrying out all this stuff they are stealing?"

The man answered, "Right over there, the door marked DO NOT LOCK."

In the meantime Chester noted that the security guard was selling eggs and honey at the security office and sending out the employees personal laundry for cleaning instead of spending his time on plant security matters.

Further investigation resulted in uncovering several other employee frauds and several were terminated. Obviously, the plant manager had no clue of what was happening in his plant, as he was too involved in outside activities.

Investigating Corporate Fraud

DISAPPEARING TAIL PIPES

A manufacturing plant in West Virginia produced tail pipes as original equipment for automobile manufacturers and for the replacement market. Over the past few months the company had experienced tail pipe inventory shortages.

Clyde was on a special assignment and was not available to participate in a review of the company operation. Chester went it alone to the plant and began a review of plant security. All sides of the plant facilities had appropriate fencing. A Guard was stationed at the employee entrance and exit to the employee parking lot. However, the back of the plant faced a railroad siding where all products were shipped to customers. A high fence was across the back of the plant. There appeared to be no way for the tail pipes to be carried out in employee cars and trucks.

The only way that product could be leaving the plant seemed to be by employees throwing tail pipes over the fence at the loading dock area at the back of the plant and onto the railroad right of way. Employees were apparently coming back to the area after dark and picking up the tail pipes. Some of the tail pipes leaving the plant were apparently to supply needs for friends of the employees.

The plant was operating on a 24-hour schedule. Chester discussed with the plant manager the make up of ages of individuals employed at the plant. He learned that many of the employees were 18 years old and still in High School. The disappearance of tail pipes seemed like something that young kids would be involved in.

Chester, over the next 24-hour three-shift period interviewed all the 18-20 year old youths about their participation or knowledge of any thefts. During the night shift, one employee admitted to knowing that four employees were stealing tail pipes. He also said one employee had a lot of tail pipes currently in the trunk of his car.

The next morning Chester discussed his findings with the plant manager. The manager was asked if he had a good friend on the police force that would do us a favor by checking out the trunk of the indicated employee. But first, Chester wanted to talk to the four youths involved. They were interviewed and each signed a confession disclosing their thefts. The policeman friend of the manager was requested to accompany the youths to the home of the indicated employee and check in his car trunk. A trunk full of tail pipes was found and taken back to the plant.

Chester called all four back to the plant for a final discussion. Chester said that he could tell these employees were basically good kids. He hated that if the employees were prosecuted, their record would follow them all their lives. The employees expressed their sorrow for what they had done. Chester told them he didn't want them to be penalized all their lives for the thefts they had made. The loss to the company was several hundred dollars and some recoveries had been made. Chester told the employees that he was

Disappearing Tail Pipes

going to recommend that the plant manager not pursue prosecution if they promised to get their lives straight and never get involved in anything like this again.

The employees promised from that time forward to go straight. Their parents were not at all happy at what their sons had done but were so appreciative of how this matter was conducted.

Chester had been told that a company airplane would be in Washington DC to bring him home if he got through with the investigation in time. Since he had been working two days straight, he told the pilots that he couldn't get to DC in time before for the airplane was scheduled to leave. It was going to take Chester at least three hours to get to the DC airport. Several company employees were already on the airplane and ready to depart. According to the pilots these people had been in DC for about three days living it up at company expense doing nothing productive. One of the pilots said, "You know I think I just found a maintenance problem with the airplane. If you hurry we should be able to fix the problem by the time you get here.

When Chester arrived at the airport in DC, surprisingly the airplane problem had just been fixed and the plane immediately departed for Houston. The other employees had been sitting on the airplane for three hours. They were not very happy to see Chester board the airplane as they suspected what the pilots had done.

Clyde and Chester had always tried to be considerate of the pilots to make their work as easy as possible. According to several of the pilots, many of the company employees were very demanding and inconsiderate. The pilots were happy to return the favor to Chester.

Not many people would have gone out of their way to make it easy for Chester to get home, as the pilots did.

THE FICTITIOUS COMPANY

Clyde and Chester were requested to conduct an audit and investigation of various plant transactions by the newly named controller of a field auto parts distribution center in one of the operating divisions.

During the course of the review, it was discovered that the assistant plant controller had padded his expense account for certain personal airplane trips; had a relocation allowance paid, when, in fact, he only moved two blocks down the street; and had purchased some office furniture which had been paid for by the division.

Through discussions with the office furniture vendor, they determined that the furniture had been purchased for a company with an address in another city although the furniture was delivered to the assistant plant controller's home address. These charges totaled about $5,000.

Since the assistant plant controller was in a position to approve and pass invoices for payment and had access to blank checks, all canceled checks for a period of time were reviewed to see if any payments had been made by the division to the company which appeared on the furniture order.

A $21,000 check had been issued to a fictitious company that had been deposited in the same city where the assistant plant controller lived.

The chief accountant of the plant resigned shortly after discovery of padded expense accounts.

Further investigation of the plant disbursements uncovered certain large checks issued to what was discovered to be a fictitious company. The checks were issued and signed with the facsimile signature plate under the control of the assistant plant controller.

The assistant plant controller had been making the bank reconciliations. Certain canceled checks were missing from the prior month's bank statements.

Copies of these checks were obtained from the bank that revealed, during a nine-month period, checks totaling $250,000 had been issued to this fictitious company and deposited in a city nearby.

Further review disclosed that the former controller of the division, assistant plant controller, and chief accountant were the recipients of the funds paid to the fictitious company established by them.

A review of the hard copy of the check filed with the cash disbursements disclosed that the payee's name had been changed prior to submittal to data processing in

The Fictitious Company

order that the fictitious company name would not appear in the division accounting records. Destruction of the canceled checks made an audit trail impossible.

Clyde confronted the individuals with the information obtained during the audit and obtained full detailed signed confessions. These confessions confirmed that the three employees were acting together in the conspiracy and all were profiting from the funds obtained.

The investigative information and signed confessions were turned over to the district attorney and all three were charged with felony theft.

All three plead guilty to the charges.

Two were sentenced to three years in the penitentiary and fined $7,500.

The third employee received a four-year sentence and a $7,500 fine. The sentence was probated conditional upon restitution of $50,000 to the insurance bonding company.

The division subsequently received $276,000 from the fidelity bond insurance claim Chester filed to recover the division's loss. The $50,000 in employee restitution was forwarded to the bonding company.

Investigating Corporate Fraud

MISSISSIPPI MUD

Clyde and Chester were requested to go to a tail pipe and muffler manufacturing plant in Mississippi that was currently closed due to union employees out on strike.

This plant had been unionized for several years but there had been few employee problems in the past.

Negotiations had started out amicably but had turned nasty during the past week. There had been several threats of violence that seemed out of character based on past experience.

The company's division office had sent a labor negotiations expert from Chicago to head up the management negotiating team.

When Clyde and Chester arrived at the plant in Mississippi they were invited to the union/management meeting being held that afternoon.

Observing discussions at the meeting, it became obvious that both sides were very hostile towards each other. The prior evening, a concrete culvert at the plant manager's home had been dynamited.

Veiled threats were being made that the plant might be blown up next. Union representatives seemed particularly hostile towards the labor negotiator from Chicago.

After the meeting broke up, Clyde and Chester went to the plant manager's office. They asked him what was going on. They wondered why negotiations had been allowed to deteriorate into such a bitter standoff.

After much coaxing, the plant manager said that the union people did not like the man from Chicago.

When asked to elaborate, he hesitated to respond thinking they were in support of the labor specialist.

They then questioned why someone from the mid-west was sent to negotiate in the south. Obviously, attitudes and sentiments in Mississippi were much different than those in Chicago.

The plant manager said he had no say in the matter. The division office sent him without the manager's request or approval. The plant manager had always conducted negotiations himself in the past without any of the problems currently being experienced.

The plant manager finally told them what was troubling the union. The labor man from Chicago had told the union during the first meeting that if the strike wasn't settled

Mississippi Mud

soon he was going to bring four or five busloads of blacks from up north to take over their jobs and operate the plant.

As this was a small all white community in southern Mississippi, this threat immediately alienated everyone present. Animosity against the plant had spread throughout the community. Clyde and Chester were outraged by what had taken place.

Later that day, they called the company's home office and passed on the information obtained. They were asked for their advice. They advised to immediately get rid of the labor negotiator from Chicago and let them try to reverse the damage he had created.

The home office agreed and the labor negotiator was advised by the division to return to Chicago immediately.

The plant was the only major employer in town and local business was dependent on the jobs provided.

By this time public opinion in the community had turned completely against the company and plant management. Rumors persisted that the plant was going to be dynamited.

Clyde and Chester began immediately to try to repair the damage. They met with union representatives and assured them that the comments made by the labor negotiator in no way represented either the feelings of local plant management or that of the home office. The union representatives were asked to start all over again with a new spirit in their negotiations with management.

Meetings were requested with the local chamber of commerce, rotary, American legion, major business owners, and churches.

They spoke at each of the meetings assuring these groups that union and management were going to get back on the same page. They apologized for the way the Chicago labor negotiator had conducted the plant negotiations. The groups were assured that everyone would benefit by an amicable solution to the strike.

Based on their apologies and assurances that the plant would conduct current and future labor negotiations in an honorable manner, union and management meetings began again and an amicable solution was reached within a week.

All the hard feelings between union and plant management and threatened violence had been triggered by the wrong kind of mud slinging in Mississippi.

AUTOMOBILE KICKBACKS

The company purchases hundreds of trucks and automobiles each year for the home office and various field offices located from Texas to Massachusetts.

Chester was asked to make a review of vehicle purchases for the last three years. Chester found that one employee in the company's purchasing department placed all vehicle requirements out for bids each year.

The review disclosed that all purchases had been made from the same local automobile dealer during each of the past three years. Since no bid records were kept, no review could be made of the bids actually submitted. However, Chester went to several local auto dealers to get their story on the annual bids. Some of the dealers said they were not allowed to bid by the company employee. Others said there was something fishy about the same dealer being the low bidder each year. One dealer said he purposely submitted an impossibly low bid that year. He knew that no one else could beat his bid price as it was below his cost. He thought our employee must have some kind of deal with that dealer.

Further review disclosed that there was no standardization of style or equipment placed on the cars and trucks, meaning the vehicles were purchased made basically to order. In many cases equipment was purchased that was not necessary for the vehicles intended usage. Vehicles required for the field operations were all supplied and shipped by the one local dealer. Trade-in vehicles were brought back to that dealer for disposition.

Chester suspected that at the very least the employee was being provided a new car every year with all service to the car included. As Chester had no evidence, he passed on his suspicions to Clyde. Clyde thought that the matter warranted follow up and he approached the employee for an interview.

During Clyde's interrogation of the employee, he admitted that he was showing favoritism to the one dealer and had received a new car each year along with other substantial perks. Obviously, the company had overpaid for each vehicle acquired. However, no recoveries wee made.

The employee was terminated. Several purchasing procedures were overhauled to prevent this occurrence in the future. Each year a committee of purchasing agents will solicit local bids for vehicle use in the home office and assign purchase orders to the low bidders. Standardized equipment will be specified so that each automobile and pick up truck will be equipped the same. Pick up trucks will now be supplied to all field locations. Arrangements were made with the vehicle district distribution centers for dealers in the appropriate locations to supply vehicles for the field operations at the same price or better that the low bidder in the home office area. New arrangements were made for the used pickups to be "traded in" at the field dealer location rather than having all vehicles shipped to the home office for trade-in.

Investigating Corporate Fraud

THE NARROW ESCAPE

Clyde and Chester were requested to perform a security review at an automobile parts manufacturing plant in northern Michigan. The company furnished a company Viscount airplane for their trip.

Clyde had made arrangements for Al, manager of a nationally renowned guard service company, to accompany them to help evaluate the guard service currently being used. Al was a good friend of both.

But first, you need to know a little about Al. Al was about 55 years old, looked very distinguished, dressed impeccably, and was very wealthy.

Al was as tight as a drum with money. One time he tipped a bellhop a whopping 50 cents for carrying 5 suitcases to his room in Las Vegas. Al is just the kind of person others love to harass.

When Chester arrived at the private airplane terminal of the company, Al was already there. Not knowing that Al was afraid of flying, Chester asked Al, "Have you checked with the pilots about the weather for the flight?"

Al said, "No."

Chester said he would go check and returning in a few minutes decided to put a story on Al.

Chester told Al, "We will be flying through some heavy turbulence about a half hour out but the pilots think they can get through it all right. However, for a while, it will be a real bumpy ride.

Chester also told Al, "The plane will be landing in a heavy snowstorm in Michigan, although it probably will not be real icy." Al began to turn a sickly white.

About that time Clyde arrived. Al relayed to Clyde what Chester had told him.

Clyde carried the story on by confirming, "That's the same story the pilot's told me."

Clyde turned to Chester and whispered that Al was scared to death of flying. He had a really hard time persuading Al to come along with them on this trip.

Al said, "I'm not going. I'm afraid of bad weather." They harassed him until finally he boarded the plane with them. The inside of the airplane was configured with two sofa seats and several reclining chairs with tables.

The Narrow Escape

Once airborne, they continued the story about the weather with Al until he said, "I'm getting sick." Clyde gave Al a Dramamine tablet.

Al laid down on one of the sofas and soon fell asleep.

Chester found a couple of blankets and large safety pins. He and Clyde covered Al with the blankets and safety-pinned him to the sofa.

When Al awoke he was sweating up a storm and was still sick. Chester went over to the food pantry on the airplane and found a tin of smoked oysters. Chester opened the smoked oysters and asked Al if he was hungry. He passed them back and forth under Al's nose. The oysters smelled terrible and Al almost heaved from the smell.

Al, noticing that he was pinned to the sofa, told Clyde and Chester, "I'm very sick. I don't know, I may die, but I'll tell you one thing. If I ever get well and get out of here, I'm going to kill you both!"

Clyde and Chester howled with laughter at Al's predicament.

Upon landing in Michigan, sure enough there was a heavy snowstorm with about eighteen inches already on the ground. The landing strip was out in the country with only a shed for a terminal. The airstrip was just long enough to accommodate the airplane.

Arriving at the plant, Clyde, Chester and Al went throughout the site reviewing and evaluating security. Although the plant manager voiced no security problems, it became obvious that very little security existed although there were several guards in place at the plant twenty-four hours a day.

The manager was asked if the plant had experienced any losses from theft. He replied that there was nothing of value at the plant to steal. Chester stated that maybe the plant should be shut down since not even the products produced are apparently of any value since you stated there was nothing at the plant worth stealing!

That night, to set an example as to how ineffective plant security was, the three drove their rental car in past the empty guard shack to the parts storage area. There appeared to be nobody working in the area although the plant operated around the clock. Opening the trunk of the car, they loaded two tires, three batteries, chain, and several other items in the back. They drove out of the plant unseen.

The next morning they drove back to the plant and told the plant manager about their "thefts" the night before and took him out to the car to see the plunder.

The plant manager was obviously shocked and agreed with their recommendations to immediately improve overall security at the plant.

When they arrived at the little terminal to leave, the airplane wheels were frozen to the ground in the ice. They all chipped the ice away and a tractor pulled the airplane out to the end of the runway. Clyde, Chester, and Al boarded the plane and prepared for take-off.

As the airplane started down the runway to take off, Chester noticed the tractor driver following them frantically waving at them to stop.

Chester shouted to the pilots, "Shut her down! Now!"

The pilots aborted the take-off, stopping just short of a huge deep, ditched area that had formerly been a gravel pit operation. The pilots got off the plane and asked the tractor operator what was the matter.

Before take off the pilots had forgotten to take the chocks out of the tail elevator and stabilizer. The airplane, had it not stopped, would not have left the ground and would have gone down into the deep gravel pit.

The pilots were white as sheets when they climbed back into the airplane and nothing more was said as everyone was pretty well shaken up.

Clyde and Chester did not have to harass Al on the way home as the departing incident had wiped him out.

But it wasn't over yet! About an hour into flight, as Chester was walking down the aisle to get a cup of coffee, there was a loud "Boom" and Chester was thrown into the side wall of the airplane.

One of the pilots came running back shouting, "What happened?"

There was a loud rush of air and looking back towards the rear of the airplane, they noticed that a side window had blown out.

There was nothing to do but to move up front and stay away from the windowless area.

Needless to say, Al never took another airplane trip with them!

UNDERCOVER IN MISSISSIPPI

The company had acquired through an acquisition of a company a plant operation in a city in Mississippi. As this plant operation was not that familiar to management, Clyde and Chester were requested to make a cursory review of the plant and go undercover so as not to alarm the local management.

Clyde asked his secretary to book rooms for Chester and himself under fictitious names, which she did.

As they arrived at their destination at the Holiday Inn, they looked at the big billboard sign in front of the motel that read, "Welcome Clyde Wilson and Chester Karrick." So much for trying to remain anonymous! They never knew how the motel got their names or why they were put on their big sign out front. At that point they did not know if the plant personnel knew where we were from or the type of work usually performed.

They advised the home office management of our reception at the motel. It was decided that they would not go to the plant or meet any of the employees. Their assignment was changed to checking the standard of living of the key personnel and to review the security for access to the plant with regards to location and effectiveness of the guards, access limitations, employee parking lots, fencing, cameras, shipment areas for company products, etc.

They were to report these findings when they returned home and schedule an above board return visit in a few months after plant disruptions settle down due to the recent acquisition and change of ownership.

They completed that review in a couple of days and reported their findings. They made arrangements to follow up on their findings and recommendations at a later date.

CHASING THE HORSES

This investigation began through suspicious actions by the controller at a Midwest company automotive parts distribution center. As this was a small office, the controller had responsibility for accounting and treasury functions. He had invoice approval authority and could sign payroll and disbursement checks.

In addition, the controller reconciled the payroll bank account and certain other bank accounts. Bank statements were sent directly to the controller from the bank.

When the home office of the company division became suspicious of certain banking activities, Clyde and Chester were asked to investigate. Their investigation disclosed the following information about the controller's activities.

The controller had acquired a fancy for the racehorses and eventually began to gamble and lose quite heavily for his station in life. In order to cover these gambling losses and meet his recurring family obligations, the controller began to convert company funds to his own use.

As the controller had sole custodial control over blank payroll checks and the signature plate used for signing payroll checks, he initiated additional payroll checks payable to himself on several occasions. As he reconciled the payroll bank statement each month, this fraud went undiscovered for several months.

The controller approved invoices for payment covering his personal purchases and caused company checks to be issued to pay for those purchases. In addition, the controller prepared various journal voucher entries whereby he accrued fictitious liabilities for office supplies, office equipment, legal, and auditing expenses.

Later, he cleared the accrual accounts through issuance of checks that he converted to cash and placed in his personal bank account. Checks issued were posted as canceled. Canceled checks, voucher daily register pages, and voucher entries were later destroyed.

The company had established a separate bank account for payment of certain costs to be incurred in making a market survey relative to possibly expanding business operations into new business territories.

In order to maintain the confidentiality of this study, the controller was instructed to handle all transactions on this account personally, including receipt of bank statements, canceled checks and subsequent bank reconciliations.

The controller took advantage of this situation to issue several unauthorized checks that he was able to convert to cash for his own use.

By the time Clyde and Chester discovered the controller's actions, he had obtained over $54,200 in company funds. In addition, the controller had destroyed virtually all company records related to this theft.

The controller was confronted by Clyde with the information uncovered in the investigation. He finally admitted the theft of company monies and gave Clyde a signed statement of confession covering his fraudulent activities.

As the controller had destroyed most of records, he was requested to bring in all his bank statements and canceled checks for the past eighteen months.

Upon receiving the financial information from the controller, the loss to the company was substantially reconstructed.

About $5,000 in restitution was obtained from the Controller and the balance of the $49,200 loss was recovered from filing a fidelity bond insurance claim.

The controller was prosecuted and sentenced to two years in prison.

THE MISSING PARTS

A company owned a truck sales dealership and service operation in the city. Many such dealerships also owned were scattered throughout the country. The company's home office was on the West Coast.

The company called Clyde and Chester to initiate an investigation when the local operation began experiencing large losses of repair parts.

They began their investigation by reviewing security over the parts storage area and how parts were issued to service personnel for repair jobs.

Controls appeared weak as any maintenance and repair employee had ready and unlimited access to the parts.

As it was probable that thefts were originating from inside the operation, they set up surveillance after working hours to watch employees as they left work for their vehicles at 5 p.m.

Some were followed from the work place. During the second evening, two company employees were observed entering a competitor's truck repair shop several blocks down the street from the company. Keeping the two employees under observation, they noticed that the company employees worked on truck repairs until about 10:00 to 11:00 pm each evening at the competitors repair shop.

Suspecting that these two employees were stealing parts for use at the competitor's truck repair shop, Clyde called the two into the office the next day for interrogation.

Faced with the suspicions and findings, the two employees finally admitted that they worked for a competitor each evening and on some weekends.

They also admitted stealing the company's truck repair parts as needed for the competitor's truck repair jobs. They in effect stole the parts as needed by the competitor for truck repairs and sold them to the competitor for about forty cents on the dollar.

Clyde obtained signed statements from the employees. They were terminated and turned over to the police. They were later tried and convicted for theft.

A complete inventory of the company's repair parts was taken based on information provided in the confessions that established the company's loss at about $72,000.

Chester assisted the company in filing a fidelity bond insurance claim to recover the loss of $72,000.

CHEMICALS, PAPER PRODUCTS, MINING

THE VENGEFUL LETTER

Most businesses receive an anonymous and or vengeful letter from time to time alleging various misdeeds by company employees.

Our experience has shown that most businesses pass off these letters as being sent by an angered spouse or troublemaker within the organization trying to throw dirt on an employee for a variety of reasons. On very few occasions are any investigations conducted and the letters just thrown in the trash.

Experience has shown that in about 95% of such cases, there is enough truth in the allegations to warrant an investigation.

Such was the case when a letter was sent to the Chairman of the Board of a large corporation. The letter was forwarded to Chester. The letter contained the following statements:

> "I have written a letter before to the President of the division where my husband works. Nothing was done.
>
> I am writing you and if you don't care, I'll forget about it.
>
> My husband bought a new Oldsmobile and Cadillac and paid cash. He made a large cash down payment on our house.
>
> He paid cash for our new furniture. He claims he lost a brief case containing over $20,000 in cash when he had a flat tire on the turnpike.
>
> He works at a plant in City A as a Purchasing and Traffic Supervisor. He makes $750 a month. I don't know what he's doing but he doesn't make enough to pay for all he has bought."
>
> Sincerely,
>
> Mrs. XYZ

After reading the letter, Chester called the company's division auditors for that plant operation and asked them to review the activities under the Purchasing and Traffic Supervisor's control to see what he might be doing.

The Vengeful Letter

They told Chester that their Division President had received a similar letter a couple of months ago.

The auditors told Chester that they had conducted a complete audit review of the Supervisor's activities and found nothing wrong. They passed off the letter as being from a vengeful, disgruntled wife.

At that time, the Plant Manager had called the Supervisor into his office and asked him about the allegations. He told the manager that he and his wife were embroiled in a nasty divorce and she was doing everything she could to embarrass him and cause him trouble.

The Plant Manager believed the Supervisor's explanation.

Chester was told by the auditors to forget it, as there was nothing to the allegations.

Chester discussed the letter with Clyde.

Clyde told Chester that he put a lot of credence in vengeful letters. Clyde's experience had taught him that there was always some truth in what the letters covered.

They felt that a further review of the allegations was warranted.

Chester called the division auditors to advise them that he and Clyde would be at the plant next week to initiate a review and they were welcome to join.

The auditors advised that such a trip was a waste of time and not to come.

Chester advised that he and Clyde would be there next week and they could join in the review or stay at home.

When they arrived at the area airport next week the auditors were there to meet them.

The home address of the Supervisor's wife was about an hours drive from the airport. They drove down to interview her.

Upon arrival, they found a black woman lying in a hammock stretched between two trees in the front yard, a glass of iced tea in her hand, and watching a black and white TV hanging from a tree.

Clyde introduced himself and the others to the woman.

She replied, "I wondered if anybody was ever going to do anything."

During the interview, she acknowledged that she and her white husband had separated. She had thrown him out of the house, as all he was interested in was kinky sex. She added that all the paraphernalia he had left in the garage could be reviewed but was told that we were not interested.

She was asked about the $20,000 in cash her husband had lost on the turnpike.

She stated that her husband was going to buy an interest in a bar upstate and had placed $20,000 in a briefcase to pay for his interest. On his way to the bar, he had a flat tire on the turnpike.

He had placed the briefcase in the car trunk. In order to get the spare tire, jack, etc. out of the car trunk, he had placed the briefcase beside the car. After changing the tire, he had placed the flat tire and jack into the trunk but had forgotten the briefcase.

After going about ten miles down the turnpike he remembered leaving the briefcase and turned around to go back to get it. However, when he got back to the spot of the flat, the briefcase was gone.

She couldn't add anything more than what was in the letter.

Chester noted that a new Oldsmobile was in the driveway. He copied the license number and information from the dealer tag onto a pad.

With still not much to go on, Clyde, Chester, and the auditors drove to the company's plant located in the next city. They drove into the parking lot right by the guard who was asleep in his chair in the guard shack. Among all the beat-up Fords and Chevrolets in the parking lot was a brand new Cadillac.

They parked by the Cadillac and decided to look inside to see what could be found. Looking in the glove compartment, Chester found a bank statement for the ABC Freight Company with a P. O. Box mailing address for a nearby city. The bank statement showed a balance of $24,135.25.

Chester also found a bank statement in a woman's name containing a street address in another city. The statement showed a bank balance of $352.15.

Chester copied the license number and dealer information from the back of the Cadillac onto a note pad.

Clyde and Chester decided to go inside the plant and introduce themselves to the Plant Manager explaining why they were there.

Inside the plant, they were advised that the plant manager was not there today. They asked to see the plant superintendent and were advised that he was playing golf that day.

The secretary was then asked who is next in charge when the manager and superintendent were not there. They were advised that the Purchasing and Traffic Supervisor was next in line of authority.

Chester told Clyde, "I guess we might as well interview him since we've come this far."

Clyde said, "What are we going to ask him as we don't even know what his duties really are?"

Chester told Clyde, "I'm sure you will think of something."

They went into the Purchasing and Traffic Supervisor's office and introduced themselves. They told the supervisor they were there to do a fraud investigation.

As Chester always carried several big file folders containing a lot of working papers, he decided to place them on the supervisor's desk.

Clyde turned to the supervisor and said, pointing at Chester, "Have you seen this man before?"

The man said, "No."

Clyde said, "He's been here for the past six weeks following your every move. He knows every time you have even gone to the bathroom. Tell him Chester a little of the background you have."

This caught Chester a little off guard, but he replied, "We know that you bought a new Oldsmobile from Dealer X in the next city and paid cash for it. We know that you paid cash for a Cadillac you bought from Dealer Y. You paid cash for new furniture. You lost over $20,000 in a brief case left along side the turnpike. You are shacking up with Ms. Z over in the next city who has a bank account at Bank B with a $352.15 balance. You have a company by the name of ABC Freight Company with an account balance of $24,135.25 in Bank C."

The supervisor said, "Damn, you do know all about me don't you."

Still not knowing what to interrogate the man about, Clyde said, " What you tell us in the next thirty minutes will determine whether you spend the next three years in jail or whether you spend ten years in jail. Take this pad and pen and describe what and how you have been stealing. If you come up with the same figure Chester has calculated in his working papers showing us that you are telling the truth, I'll see that you only get three years in jail."

The supervisor took the pad and pen and started writing. They looked at each other as the man continued to write several pages. When he finished, he handed his statement to Clyde to read.

Clyde turned to Chester and said that the supervisor had admitted stealing $121,315.85. Clyde then asked Chester, "Does this agree with your numbers?"

Chester opened up his mock files and scanned through a few pages and replied to Clyde, "That number is close enough."

Clyde then got the supervisor to sign over the Cadillac title to the company. The supervisor also assigned his savings account and bank account to the company. This provided restitution of about $45,000.

Chester then called the police to come out to the plant. Clyde gave the policeman a copy of the statement that the supervisor had written. The policeman was asked to take a similar statement from the supervisor. This would give the police all that was needed to arrest the man. The supervisor was fired and then taken to jail.

Based on the information given in the statement, the auditors could then corroborate the loss from the company's books to aid in the prosecution.

Based on the supervisor's statement, his fraud was reconstructed. The company had adopted a bank freight payment plan whereby a central bank in another state made payments directly to the freight carriers. The supervisor twice a month batched the freight carrier invoices together with copies of the bills of lading and transmitted them to the bank for payment. Such practice eliminated the necessity of company personnel handling the freight payment function and helped in cash management.

Periodically, the bank transmitted a statement seeking reimbursement for amounts paid. Copies of the paid freight bills and bills of lading were transmitted in support.

After review at the division office, each plant was sent its respective batch of paid freight invoices. The plant reviewed the paid freight invoices and maintained the files.

All freight audits were to be made after payment, although it was later found post audit procedures had broken down.

The payment plan did not hold the bank responsible for paying only invoices that corresponded to an approved company vendor name and address list.

At this plant, the freight and traffic section consisted of the supervisor and a female clerk. The plant shipped half of its product by company trucks and half by common carrier that meant that company monthly freight costs should be fairly the same.

The Vengeful Letter

The purchasing and traffic supervisor selected the carrier, scheduled the truck movements, prepared the bills of lading, received the only copy of the guard log reflecting vehicle movements, and maintained the paid freight invoice files and plant copies of the bills of lading.

The supervisor took advantage of the internal control weaknesses through manipulating the paperwork and submitting fraudulent invoices by his fictitious freight company.

The supervisor invented a fictitious name for a freight carrier; printed freight invoices; obtained a post office box in another city; and opened a bank account in another city in the name of the his fictitious company.

On certain freight shipments of product by company truck, the supervisor placed a piece of paper between the carbon and the freight carrier's copy of the bill of lading in order that the carrier's name would not print on such copy when the bill of lading was typed.

Later he typed in the name of his fictitious company on the carrier's copy of the bill of lading and prepared a freight invoice to the company covering the shipment. Several shipments would be handled in this manner over a two or three day period.

The supervisor then prepared a batch transmittal covering these freight invoices and forwarded them to the central bank for payment. Upon receipt of the bank's check at his post office box, the employee made deposits into the bank account of his fictitious company.

This scheme continued undetected as the supervisor destroyed the guard log and destroyed the paid invoices when returned to the plant. As a further breakdown in internal controls, customer invoices were not being matched to the freight bills and bills of lading.

The supervisor had been using this system for about ten months during which time he had stolen over $121,315.85.

Another sign that no one in management was watching the store as freight expense had more that doubled over the past six months. The company's plant operating monthly expense statements reflected the substantial increased cost of freight and should have been investigated by management.

They returned home that night having proved again that there is truth in vengeful letters.

A fidelity bond insurance claim was filed to cover the remaining $76,315.85 loss to the company.

THE STRIKING EXPERIENCE

Clyde and Chester were sent to the East Coast to conduct a security review at an old chemical plant.

Upon arriving at the plant, there was very little work activity as they found that plant employees were on strike. They learned that this location had been experiencing labor problems on an ongoing basis.

In the security review, they surveyed plant perimeter fencing, guard locations and instructions, personnel and employee access, security camera positioning, employee parking lot locations and access, and procedures for searching incoming and outgoing vehicles among many other security matters providing necessary plant security.

After finishing the security review, they were invited to sit in on a labor-management negotiations meeting. At issue was apparently an ongoing strike over labor demands for a one-dollar to a one-dollar and a quarter per hour pay increase.

After listening to the heated barbs back and forth for a few hours, they were asked by a union man what they thought about the situation.

Clyde asked Chester, "Is this plant making any money?"

Chester replied, "This plant makes very little money and has been a source of continued labor discontent."

Chester stated, "If this plant strike isn't settled in another week, the plant could possibly be shut down permanently."

The union people took issue with that statement and made several veiled threats that the plant might very well mysteriously be dynamited or set afire.

Chester stated, "We are more than adequately insured. If you plan on setting fire or blowing up the plant go ahead; do us a favor."

In a few minutes, the meeting broke up. Returning to their motel room after eating dinner, they received a telephone call.

Clyde answered the phone. A gravelly voice on the other end of the line stated that if he was paid $100,000 the strike could be settled immediately. He was emphatically told that no payments would ever be made. Veiled threats were made again to the effect that there might not be any plant there next week.

He was told that the plant was more than adequately insured and to go ahead and do whatever he planned to do.

The Striking Experience

The man was also told that in any case if the strike wasn't settled soon it appeared that management might shut down the plant permanently.

As they had probably exceeded their authority in this matter, they thought it wise to contact the parent company about what had been said.

The company CEO was apprised of the situation. He agreed with what they had done. He also felt that if any payment was made to union people to settle the strike that this would just be the first in a line of continued demands for more and more money.

Later that night, they received another telephone call at their motel room. A man on the other end of the line told them to go to a particular Catholic church tomorrow afternoon, which was Saturday, at 2:30 pm.

They were advised to sit in the middle of the pew on the fourth row on the right side of the chapel. No other information was given. They agreed to be at the chapel.

The next afternoon they went to the chapel and sat in the fourth row as directed and observed what appeared to be a mob funeral. Flowers were everywhere.

After they were seated and about two-thirds through the funeral service, a big burly man came in and sat on Chester's right. In a few minutes, an elderly, short, well-dressed man came in and sat down on Clyde's left. The whole scene appeared to be something out of the "Godfather".

Nothing was said until the funeral was almost over.

The man on Clyde's left whispered to Clyde, "What will you give me; I've got to have something!"

Clyde told him that the plant would increase the union pay by twenty-five cents an hour but they had to be at work by 7:00 am Monday morning. The man stuck out his hand and shook Clyde's hand. Nothing more was said.

Monday morning all plant personnel showed up for work at 7:00 am and that was the end of the unusual and strange circumstances surrounding the plant strike.

Investigating Corporate Fraud

CORNED BEEF AND CABBAGE

Clyde and Chester went to the Mid-west to investigate possible inventory shortages in a company paint, dye and colors plant operation. The plant manager was suspected of being involved in fraud.

The plant manager was asked to meet with Clyde and Chester at a motel a few blocks from the plant at 2:00 pm that afternoon.

They had arrived in the city about 11:00 am that morning and checked into the motel. As this was several hours before the manager arrived, they went to the motel restaurant for lunch. The luncheon special that day was corned beef and cabbage.

Clyde quickly said he wanted the luncheon special.

Chester said, "Clyde, you know you have a spastic colon. Corned beef and cabbage will tear you up."

Clyde replied, "No sweat, I'll be all right."

Clyde ordered the corned beef and cabbage and Chester ordered a BLT.

Over lunch they realized the need for a secretary that could take shorthand and type the statement that would be taken.

Chester went to the motel office to see if someone there could help them around 2:00 pm that afternoon. The motel clerk introduced Chester to a young lady who said she would help. She was told to come to the room at 2:00 pm.

The plant manager and the young lady arrived about the same time and were asked to take seats around the table in the room.

The girl got out her shorthand pad ready for taking a statement. Clyde turned his charm on the manager.

The manager persistently denied any involvement in the inventory shortages. After about ten or fifteen minutes the manager started crying and began telling Clyde about his thefts.

Clyde started dictating a statement to the young lady. Every few minutes she furiously scratched her upper body. This was distracting.

Finally, Chester asked her, "What is the problem?"

185

Corned Beef And Cabbage

She replied, "Several friends and I spent last Saturday in Aspen skiing naked in the snow. I got sunburned and am now peeling all over."

Chester told her to go back to her office, as they didn't need her anymore. Chester told Clyde that he would write the statement out in longhand on a notepad.

Just as Clyde started dictating the statement again, he excused himself. The corned beef and cabbage had just taken effect. He headed for the bathroom.

By the time Clyde returned to the room, the plant manager had regained his composure. He didn't want to talk anymore. Clyde confronted him again with the plant losses. In a few minutes the manager began to cry again. He then began to tell Clyde again all about his thefts.

Just at that time Clyde had to excuse himself again.

When Clyde returned, they had to start the procedure all over again. Just as Chester started writing the statement Clyde excused himself again.

When Clyde didn't return in a few minutes, Chester told the manager to get his chair and pull it over in front of the bathroom door. Chester also pulled his chair over to the door.

Chester then kicked the bathroom door open and there sat Clyde in the lavatory sink splashing cold water up on his behind. The corned beef and cabbage had not only given him diarrhea but also aggravated his hemorrhoids.

Clyde yelled, "What is going on?"

Chester replied, "If this statement is ever going to be finished we figured we will have to join you."

There they all three sat while Clyde dictated and Chester wrote in longhand the manager's statement.

The manager was married and had three children living at home. He just wasn't making enough money to meet his family's demands.

The plant where the manager worked was open five days a week. During the weekend, the manager went to the plant and loaded his car with various dyes, colors, and paint.

At various times during the week the manager went by plant customer offices and offered to sell the products at a special discount price for cash. The manager had converted about $90,000 in plant products into $45,000 in cash during the past nine months.

Afraid that his wife might find out about his activities, the manager stored his ill-gotten gains in shoeboxes hidden in the bottom of his closet.

Going to the manager's home, they reclaimed about $11,000 that remained in the closet. The plant manager was terminated.

The client advised that he did not wish to pursue prosecution.

The fidelity bond insurance carried by the company had a deductible higher than the loss that precluded recovering the company's remaining loss.

PINE STUMP SHORTAGES

The company had a naval stores plant operation deep in the woods of Louisiana. Clyde and Chester were asked to review the procedures for purchasing virgin pine stumps. The company suspected some stump inventory shortages.

Arriving on the site they noted a huge pile of stumps 20 feet high and over 60 yards long. Getting an accurate inventory of the weight of the stumps and value was impossible for them. Applying the usual procedure of taking the starting inventory plus purchases less amount transferred to production to balance against ending inventory was not very accurate.

A review was made of the purchases of virgin pine stumps during the past 12 months. The company had four employees purchasing stumps. The review included matching prices paid by each employee.

The stumps were purchased based on the amount of weight on truck deliveries. The pine trees in the area were being harvested to obtain the lumber. The company bought the stumps from these harvesters, as they had no use for stumps.

The company processed the stumps to obtain turpentine, pine oil, and other naval stores products.

Since they had generated no information useful in the investigation it became a matter for Clyde to interrogate the four purchasing employees. Clyde, during the interrogation of the fourth employee, learned that one employee had a deal with one of the trucking firms to submit fraudulently weight tickets. The company had no scales on the premises and had to rely on the weights by a supposedly independent outside firm. These weights were used to validate receipt of an invoice submitted by the truckers and subsequently paid by the company. No stumps were delivered and the trucking company had received payments on their invoices. The trucking firm was splitting the invoice amount with the employee. The employee admitted that he had reported about three fake deliveries a month for about a year that resulted in a loss to the company of about $70,000.

They also discovered that the independent outside firm was not being used for the weight tickets fraudulently submitted. The trucking firm had its own scales and was using them to print the fraudulent weight tickets submitted to the company.

Clyde recovered $ 5,000 from the employee who was then terminated. Clyde notified the trucking firm of the company's intent to pursue prosecution. To avoid prosecution, the trucking company paid the remaining loss of $ 65,000. With payment by the trucking firm the company had recovered the loss amount.

THE STRAYING MATTRESSES

Based on a request from a chemical division, Clyde and Chester traveled to the East Coast to check on a suspected inventory shortage at a mattress factory.

The mattress factory was located in a small city. Driving around the area, they noticed only two or three apartment buildings, a motel, a grocery store, gas station, and two furniture stores.

Arriving at the plant, Chester reviewed the customer sales list while Clyde looked at security relating to mattress storage, shipping and delivery areas.

Chester found that all shipments of mattresses were being made primarily to out of state customers.

Reviewing their findings, they felt that mattresses were being stolen from the plant and sold locally at discount prices. It didn't seem logical that there were no sales locally or in nearby areas.

While Chester reviewed local real estate records, Clyde visited the local furniture stores.

When Chester discovered that the plant manager owned an interest in the only motel in town, he went to the motel and rented a room. The mattress in that room had come from the plant. As the maids were still cleaning rooms, he was able to slip in and check the mattresses in several of the rooms. All the rooms checked contained mattresses produced at the plant.

Clyde visited the two local furniture stores and found that each had plant manufactured mattresses for sale.

Since a review of the plant customer sales list did not reveal any local sales, they concluded that the plant manager must be involved in the thefts.

Arriving back at the plant, they noted that there was only one pickup in the employee parking lot. They bet that the plant manager owned that pickup. Clyde sought out the plant manager and confronted him with their suspicions.

After continued denials, the manager finally admitted to loading mattresses onto his truck on weekends for delivery to the local furniture stores where he sold them for half-price. He also admitted in his signed statement that he had stolen the mattresses that were used to furnish his motel.

Chester reviewed the inventory and production records and determined the client's loss to be about $52,000. About $10,000 in restitution was recovered from the plant manager. He was then turned over to the authorities for prosecution. The company's loss was less than the fidelity bond insurance deductible and no recovery was made of the remaining loss.

STAY AWAY FROM THE FIREWATER

The manager of a paper processing plant located in the Mid-West called Clyde and Chester for help in investigating suspected arsons at his plant. Two days ago a suspicious fire had started at the rear of the plant. They agreed to help.

The plant manager was told to get a video camera in case another fire occurred. The video would provide for filming all of the spectators that came to observe the fire. The film could later be scanned for the presence of current or former employees. Clyde's experience had taught him that the perpetrator of the fire usually returned to watch the burn.

A few days later Clyde and Chester arrived at the plant. The previous night another fire had occurred at the plant. The plant manager had filmed the proceedings as instructed.

Chester began reviewing all of the personnel files to identify any employees terminated within the past six months.

In the meantime, Clyde and the plant manager reviewed the films to list the names of current and former employees observing the plant fires.

Eight employees were identified by Chester as being terminated within the past six months. Three had been terminated within the past three weeks.

The plant was located near an Indian reservation. About one-half of the plant employees lived on the reservation. The three most recent terminations were Indians from the reservation. Two of the three individuals were also identified in the films being reviewed by the plant manager and Clyde.

That night, another fire was started at the plant. Again, the spectators were filmed.

The next afternoon Chester went to all of the bars in the area frequented by the local Indians in an attempt to establish if any of the three prime suspects were at a bar on the evenings before the fires had occurred.

One Indian was identified as having been in the same bar on each of the three nights prior to the fires being started.

The bartender said, "What you hear about Indians and firewater must be true. After 2 or 3 beers, this guy would appear drunk and get loud and obnoxious. I would have to get him out of here before he got in trouble."

Stay Away From The Firewater

On the two occasions that the fires had been filmed, the same Indian was observed at the front of the spectator group.

The next morning the Indian suspect was called to the plant to sign final insurance papers.

Upon arrival at the plant, the Indian was called into the plant manager's office and interrogated by Clyde. The Indian had been fired the week before for coming to work drunk. He had come to the plant drunk on two prior occasions. He finally admitted that he had started the fires as revenge for being fired.

He stated that after drinking two or three beers the more he thought about getting fired the angrier he got. He was determined to get even with everybody at the plant.

The Indian then gave Clyde a signed statement covering his criminal activity.

The Indian was then placed in jail. He just couldn't hold his firewater. No recoveries of the plant loss could be made.

SUSPECTED NAVAL STORES FRAUD

After our review of the naval stores operation in Louisiana, management requested that a similar review be made of the virgin pine stump purchases at the naval stores plant operation in Florida.

Clyde and Chester discussed the details necessary for a review of possible fraud at that location and it was decided that Chester and one of the home office auditors would go to the plant and make a preliminary review of all stump purchases. Clyde would join them after the review was complete.

Beginning the review, it was found that all stump purchases had been made by one employee for the last 20 years or more. Certainly the opportunity existed for fraud. Local management was informed of our purpose in the review. They informed us that the employee had been there for many years, was a very good employee, and there had never been a reason to suspect any irregularities. However, local management agreed that the review was necessary to remove any suspicions surrounding his work.

The auditor and Chester reviewed all the purchase orders for the past several years and found no irregularities in the paper trail. The individual whose work we were reviewing called Chester into his office one day. He told Chester that he knew what we were doing there. He stated that he had never defrauded the company in any of his business dealings and would cooperate with any investigations of him that we felt necessary.

Chester called Clyde and discussed the status of the review to date and that no evidence of possible was found in the paper work. Clyde suggested that they then look into the employee's standard of living. He said they should ask for his bank statements for the past three years, review his tax returns for the same period, and review the contents of his deposit box.

The employee was very cooperative and presented us with his last three years bank statements, stock transactions, income information, and tax returns. He took Chester to his bank to look at the safe deposit contents.

A review of his lifestyle showed that the employee was living well within his income. Nothing out of the ordinary was found in the tax returns, safe deposit box or bank statements.

A call was made to Clyde reporting that nothing out of the ordinary was found in the review of his personal records. They told Clyde that the employee had been very cooperative and knew what we were trying to prove. Clyde stated that if the employee was so cooperative, request that he take a polygraph test.

The employee was asked if he would take a polygraph test and he willingly agreed. The polygraph test disclosed no evidence of any fraud.

Suspected Naval Stores Fraud

    We congratulated the employee on performing his duties in such an exemplary fashion and thanked him for his cooperation. Management was told the details of our review. They were appreciative of the manner in which the review was conducted and pleased that the purchasing function was without any disclosed fraud.

THE COURTHOUSE SETUP

A creosote plant located in the deep redneck south was experiencing a substantial increase in costs for maintenance tools and equipment over the past year. Clyde and Chester were requested to investigate this matter.

Arriving on the scene, they surveyed the maintenance shop and storage area for tools and equipment. A maintenance manager supervised the maintenance shop.

Clyde began interviewing the maintenance employees while Chester tried to determine what items were missing and their value.

During one of the interviews, a maintenance employee mentioned that about a month ago he had seen a welding machine in the workshop at the maintenance manager's home.

In checking the records and through discussions with other employees, they found that the welding machine had been missing from the plant for about nine months.

They concluded that if the maintenance manager had the welding machine, he probably had taken many more items of tools and equipment from the plant.

The maintenance manager was called into the office and Clyde began interrogating him. He admitted that he had "borrowed" the welding machine. He agreed to go to his home with Clyde, Chester, and the plant manager to recover the welding machine.

When they arrived at the country home and went to the maintenance manager's personal workshop, they found the welding machine.

The plant manager started looking around the shop and found that there were more plant tools there than the plant had in the maintenance shop. The maintenance manager had fully equipped his shop with tools and equipment from the plant.

Confronted with these facts, the man admitted having taken all the tools and equipment in his shop from the plant over a two-year period.

While Chester inventoried the tools and equipment, Clyde took a signed statement from the maintenance manager, terminated him, and then called the police.

The estimated value of the tools and equipment stolen by the maintenance manager totaled over $ 55,000.

The police took the man to jail and impounded the plant tools and equipment as evidence for the trial.

The Courthouse Setup

Several months later when a trial date was set, the plant manager asked that either Clyde or Chester attend the trial.

Chester and an attorney went to the location the morning of the trial and checked into a local motel.

They drove around the city to locate the courthouse where the trial would take place that afternoon. Looking in the rear view mirror, Chester noticed that a police car had been following them around town.

Chester suggested that they return to the motel. Upon arriving at the motel, Chester called the plant manager to find out if anything had occurred since their investigation.

The plant manager advised that a local election had taken place since the investigation. The newly elected district attorney and judge were brothers-in-law of the former maintenance manager. The current chief of police was a cousin of the former maintenance manager.

The plant manager told Chester it appeared that the case would not be successfully prosecuted. The relatives would see that the former maintenance manager would not be convicted.

The plant manager farther advised that the local police were hopeful Chester and Clyde would show up for the trial. The local police planned to trump up some charges to put them in jail.

Thanking the plant manager for the information, Chester and the attorney checked out of the motel and quietly slipped out of town. They didn't want to be the only ones to go to jail in that little old red neck town over a company employee's theft.

THE UNDERCOVER MAN

The company owned and operated a colemanite mining operation just inside the California state line in Death Valley. Suspecting thefts of materials and supplies, the company requested that Clyde and Chester review the operation.

As they were currently tied up on other matters, they decided to use an undercover man to observe the operation until they could review the matter in person.

They did not as a practice use undercover operatives as it often could be very time consuming and expensive to the client. Results could not always be predictable.

In the oil and gas section of this book, a truck driver had stolen oil from production tanks and hidden stacks and stacks of one hundred dollar bills in his freezer.

When that case was finished, the truck driver told them he thought he would make a good investigator and wondered how he could get in the business. He begged to work with them.

Clyde thought it would be a good idea to engage this man as an undercover man in the mining operation by getting him a job at the mine site.

The former truck driver was contacted and told to get some old, beat up clothes and shoes, hitch a ride into Death Valley, and get a job at the mine operation.

He agreed as he thought this would be fun. He successfully arrived on the scene and obtained a job in the parts depot.

At the end of every week he called to report on his suspicions and findings.

Soon he started to complain about the weather and wondered when they were going to be there so he could leave. It was summertime in Death Valley and the temperatures approached 118 to 120 degrees during the day. Summer is miserable there.

After about a month Clyde and Chester left for Death Valley. They flew to Las Vegas and rented a car to journey to Death Valley.

Arriving late in the afternoon in a "town" called Furnace Creek, they decided to spend the night and go on early the next morning to the mine location.

At Furnace Creek there was only an old 8 or 10 room motel and a nearby small building called an opera house. Entering the office of the motel, they noticed that the owner was frying potatoes and onions over an open fire on the dirt floor.

Chester asked, "Do you have any vacancies for tonight?"

The owner turned to his wife and said, "I don't know about number six, as Ralph likes to stay there when he visits."

Chester asked, "Does Ralph have a reservation for tonight?"

The owner said, "No, but he likes to stay in number six when he stays here."

Chester asked, "How long has it been since Ralph was last here?"

The owner replied, "Oh, about six weeks."

Chester said, "I don't see any other cars in the parking lot. You must have some other rooms available."

The owner and his wife talked among themselves for a little while and finally said, "I guess you can have number seven and eight if you are only going to be here one night."

Chester thought that was awfully nice of them as it was obvious that no one else was going to be staying there that night and probably not for the next several weeks.

Entering their rooms, it was obvious that very few people stayed in that God forsaken place, as it was old and dirty.

As evening came, they went next door to the "opera house." The building was open and looked like an old country church with several rows of pews on either side of the aisle. Stage curtains walled off a large stage in front. Reportedly, a former renowned opera diva had settled in the area. She had built the "opera house" in order to have a place to continue to perform various operas that she had reportedly starred in the New York City area.

She performed about twice a week and only occasionally had a few attendees. She had painted the walls with bench seats.

Men and women had been painted in the bench seats so that it appeared when she sang that the house was full of people. Fortunately, she was not scheduled to perform that night.

Going to bed and asleep early, Chester was shortly awakened by the braying of a donkey which had been tied by someone to a railing just outside his room. This went on for quite awhile which kept Chester awake.

After finally falling asleep, Chester was again awakened this time by finding his bed soaked with water. A thunderstorm had peppered the area with heavy rain. The roof apparently had several major holes that had allowed the rain to leak through onto Chester's bed.

He got dressed and spent the rest of the night sleeping in the rental car. This was probably the first time this area had seen rain in several years and they had to pick that one night to be there.

The next morning they proceeded to the site of the mining operation. Upon arrival they noticed several young beautiful women, about 20 years of age, deeply tanned, and driving huge pieces of earth moving equipment. The wheels on the equipment appeared to be ten to twelve feet in diameter. Later they found out that these women were chorus dancers or prostitutes from Las Vegas who were taking a few months off from their "professional" duties to rest and gain a good tan. The girls usually were at the company bar every night. However, they didn't have anything to do with the men who worked there, which drove the men crazy.

Clyde and Chester met with their undercover man to find out what he had learned while employed at the site. The former truck driver had suspected that thefts of materials and supplies from the parts storage room were negligible.

He believed, though, that purchase orders were being issued for major purchases, invoices subsequently paid, but no deliveries made of the materials and equipment ordered.

This indicated that a company employee had made a deal with one or more Las Vegas supplier companies to obtain kickbacks or split the proceeds from this activity.

Chester began checking various purchase orders against warehouse receipts and inventory records and found many items reportedly purchased but not received.

Clyde called in the purchasing agents and confronted them with the evidence and suspicions. Signed statements were obtained from two purchasing agents who admitted that they had made a deal with two Las Vegas suppliers whereby they would issue purchase orders for items of materials and equipment. No deliveries were made against these purchase orders. When the company paid the invoices, the supplier companies split the money with the purchasing agents.

The company had incurred a loss of about $45,000 from these fraudulent activities. The employees were unable to make any restitution and were terminated.

The former trucker expressed his pleasure with his involvement in the investigation. He wanted to continue working with Clyde and Chester, but not in the desert area, as it was much too hot. The truck driver returned home, and although he frequently called Clyde for new assignments, he was never used again.

The Undercover Man

They left for Las Vegas to confront personnel of the supplier companies. On their way Clyde complained of being hungry.

They approached a grimy looking cafe in the middle of nowhere and Clyde wanted to stop. Inside the dirty looking place Clyde ordered chili.

Chester told Clyde, "You can't eat the chili here. You don't know how long it has been setting out. You will get sicker than a dog."

Clyde replied, "No way. I'm hungry for chili."

Chester reluctantly ordered a piece of apple pie and ice cream figuring that probably wouldn't make him sick.

Sure enough after they left the cafe and were about 50 miles from Las Vegas, Clyde complained of being sick.

They had to wait a day or two for Clyde to get over his bout with the chili before they could confront the suppliers.

After Clyde recovered, they approached personnel of the two supplier companies. Faced with threatened prosecution, the companies agreed to make restitution of the $45,000 loss to the company and they returned home without eating any more chili.

THE BOMB THREAT

A northeastern paper manufacturing plant, employing several hundred employees, had received bomb threat telephone calls on two occasions. After each call, the plant had been evacuated while the plant area was searched for a bomb. In each case no bomb was found and production lost for almost an entire shift.

Clyde and Chester were requested to investigate.

Arriving early one morning, they met the plant manager and requested a summary of each bomb threat telephone call.

The plant manager stated that each call came in to the plant switchboard. The message given the switchboard operator was, "There is a bomb placed in the plant." The switchboard operator reported the telephone call to the plant manager who advised his supervisors to have all employees vacate the plant for the rest of that work shift. On each of the two days the telephone calls were received, the weather was warm and beautiful.

Chester speculated, "It sounds like some employee just wanted a day off to go fishing."

Clyde advised the manager, "Let's get a tape recorder and place it at the switchboard so that the operator can record any subsequent telephone calls." A tape recorder was obtained and placed at the switchboard. As fate would have it, a bomb threat was received and recorded late that morning.

The plant manager was advised of the telephone call. The recorder and tape were taken to his office.

Thinking that the telephone call was made by a plant employee, Clyde advised the plant manager, "Have all your supervisors come in and we will listen to the tape to see if anyone recognizes the caller's voice."

When all the supervisors arrived, the tape was played several times.

Chester asked, "Does anyone recognize the caller's voice?"

Finally, after playing the tape back several times, one of the supervisors spoke up, "It sounds like one of the guys on my day shift."

Clyde advised the supervisor, "Bring in that employee." The others were dismissed.

When the identified employee arrived, Clyde took him into another office where he was interrogated about the bomb threat.

The Bomb Threat

After some conversation, the employee admitted that he had placed all three telephone calls. His girlfriend worked at the plant. He had made the calls hoping that the plant would be evacuated and they would have the day off to spend together. A statement was taken from the employee acknowledging his actions.

The plant manager was advised of the statement. The plant manager decided against pursuing prosecution but terminated the employee.

In subsequent discussions Clyde and Chester had with the plant manager, Clyde advised experience had taught that telephone bomb threats made which were non-specific were usually a ruse. But, if a telephone call was very specific, such as, "There is a bomb placed in the warehouse behind the valves and fittings set to go off at 10:30 AM." This type of call should be taken very seriously. It would then be wise to vacate the plant and notify the proper authorities.

They left to return home. The plant manager was very happy with such an early solution to his bomb threat.

ONE COAL NIGHT

Chester received a telephone call from an employee at plant in Ohio that produced Kraft paper. He requested a review of the boiler fuel utilization at their plant.

The BTU's produced from burning coal to produce steam used in the production cycle had greatly decreased in the past three months. Plant personnel had been unable to find the cause of the lower production of BTU's.

After checking into their motel room late in the evening, Clyde and Chester decided to go to the plant site that night to get a general knowledge of the plant operation.

It was a very cold night with snow and sleet on the ground and a heavy snow in the air. They arrived at the plant about 10:00 pm and drove up to the guardhouse at the plant entrance gate. They got out of the rental car and approached the guard.

Identifying themselves, they asked the guard to show them where delivery trucks unloaded coal.

The guard pointed towards the back of the plant where they noted a large pile of coal.

The guard told them all coal was delivered to that location. As needed to heat the boilers, a front-end loader brought coal to the chute at the side of the building where the coal went into the furnaces to stoke the boilers.

The plant was purchasing coal from several local coal companies.

While the guard was talking to them, a coal truck arrived at the guardhouse. The guard checked the truck bed to verify it contained a full load of coal and directed the truck inside the plant.

They noted that this truck unloaded in front of the chute leading to the furnaces inside the building.

When the truck left, Chester asked, "Why did that truck unload by the building instead of out back at the coal pile?"

The guard said, "That was done so that coal would be in position to be pushed into the furnaces when the plant opened the next morning."

After further questioning, the guard acknowledged that the firm that had just delivered coal always delivered at night. Furthermore, those trucks always unloaded by the building, not at the coal pile in the back.

One Coal Night

They walked through the cold, ice and snow to the coal pile.

Chester crawled up onto the coal pile and dug down through the frozen coal with his hands. After scraping off the top layer of coal, Chester found that there was nothing but coal slack remaining in the pile. Coal slack is scrap coal tailings and powdered coal with very low heating value.

It appeared that the truck had been loaded with a thin layer of coal on the bottom with the coal slack loaded on top. A thin layer of coal was then placed on top. When the trucker unloaded the coal, the pile looked to be only solid coal. Obviously when that pile of coal went into the boilers, low BTU's were produced due to low heat generation by the coal.

At that point, they didn't know if a plant employee was in collusion with that trucking firm or if the trucking firm owner was acting alone to defraud the plant.

The next morning they drove to the plant and conveyed their findings to the plant manager.

Learning that the purchasing manager was responsible for purchasing the coal requirements for the plant, they reviewed all purchase orders and contracts covering coal purchases. The terms of all the purchase orders and contracts were essentially the same. Coal was being purchased from five different firms.

The purchasing manager was called into the office for Clyde to interview. After reviewing the findings with the purchasing manager, Clyde concluded that the man knew nothing about the fraud.

The plant manager was asked to place a value on the loss from deliveries by the involved coal supplier. The loss was calculated to be $78,345.

The owner of the coal supplier company that had delivered coal the previous evening was called to the plant. When confronted by Clyde with their findings and the loss, the owner confessed to his involvement and gave Clyde a signed statement covering his company's fraudulent activities.

The owner agreed to reimburse the plant for the loss if prosecution was not pursued. The plant manager agreed but the coal contract was canceled.

By arriving at and observing the plant area the night before their scheduled review, Clyde and Chester had by chance uncovered the fraud in record time.

COLD COAL REVIEW

Clyde and Chester were requested to go to Montana in the middle of winter to make an appropriate review of the coal leasing operations. They arrived in Montana to find temperatures at least 20 degrees below zero. They had put on all the clothes they owned but were still freezing. The snow was deep. The roads were icy and dangerous. Arriving at the office the temperature inside must have been at least 85 degrees.

Certain areas in the state of Montana were shown to have possible extensive coal deposits and competition was great in the pursuit of land leases. Many leases had been acquired or were in the process to being acquired by the company's leasing agents. The company and its competitors had experienced fraud elsewhere in conjunction with obtaining oil leases. They were all concerned that the same situation might be occurring here.

The temperatures were so severe that pursuing interviews with ranchers from which the land leases had been obtained was not practical. Due to the weather conditions, no lease activity was being pursued at that time. The company's five lease agents were currently all in the local office.

Clyde and Chester reviewed all the lease files. Nothing in the lease files looked suspect. Not being able to pursue investigations in the field that they normally performed, they could not readily determine if any fraud had occurred.

The leasing agents were asked and all agreed to take polygraph tests. No irregularities were noted in the tests and no apparent fraud had been committed. The review was thus completed.

Clyde and Chester were both overjoyed to return to nice warm Texas.

FARMING AND PRODUCE

SEX AND THE LAND DEALS

While out of town conducting a review of a segment of a companies farming operation, Chester overheard an employee talking about land sales made by the company during the past year.

Having a particular interest in land development and sales, Chester asked the company auditors to get several of the land sale files.

The company owned a large section of land. The land was divided into 1,000-acre irrigated parcels leased to tenants for farming.

In reviewing the six land sale files, Chester noted that all sales had been made to tenants who had farmed the land for 20 years or more. What really seemed strange though was that a six percent commission had been paid to a local real estate agent on each sale.

Sales to tenants under these circumstances certainly did not appear to warrant a realtor being involved or commissions being paid.

Further review disclosed that the same realtor was involved in each transaction.

Chester noted that the division land manager initiated the documentation prepared to authorize the land sales. Furthermore, the documents contained signature approvals by the company's division executive vice-president and president.

Chester then reviewed the division policy and procedures manual covering land sales. The policy specified that absolutely no land sales were to be made through realtors as such sales could readily be made to current land tenants. There was a waiting list of tenant farmers desiring to purchase the land they were renting.

When approached about their signature approvals on the land sales, the executives said that they just had not paid any attention to the documents they signed. They agreed, however, that no sales commissions should have been paid.

A call to the local real estate board revealed that the agent was a young woman who worked out of her home.

Further background checks revealed that she was a beautiful young divorcee who lived alone in her real estate office/home, had no children, and very few real estate clients. She had been in business less than two years.

Chester advised Clyde that it appeared that the client's land manager might be getting kick-backs from the real estate agent on each land sale.

Clyde initiated a background check on the land manager. The check disclosed that the man was divorced and had three children who were living at home with him. The manager did not appear to be living beyond his salary.

Clyde asked the land manager to come in for an interview. He discussed our suspicions with the land manager but he denied getting any money from the land sales.

He acknowledged that he personally knew the real estate agent and found her very attractive.

Clyde then asked him to bring in all his bank statements and canceled checks for the past two years for our review. In reviewing his banking activity, Chester found no extraneous income.

The land manager further acknowledged having a bank safe deposit box. Chester accompanied him to the lock box. Nothing was found which related to the investigation.

Clyde then asked the land manager to take a polygraph test on the matter and he agreed.

The polygraph test confirmed that the suspect had not received any money related to the land sales but the rest of the test was inconclusive. This indicated that the suspect was withholding some information.

After further interrogation, the land manager finally admitted that he was infatuated with the real estate agent but that she would not go out with him. He admitted that the only time she would see him was when one of his land sales handled by the agent closed. He said that she slept with him on each of those occasions.

This was pretty expensive sex as it cost the company about $60,000 in real estate commissions each time a sale was completed.

Since the client's division officers had approved the land sales and the land manager received only sex for his actions, the company chose not to pursue prosecution.

CLIPPING THE CO-OP

A trucking co-op on the West Coast moved agriculture products to market for the 20 or more co-op owners. Agriculture farmers in the area formed the co-op in order to have a fixed and stable transportation source for moving their products to market. The co-op had grown to be a sizable business operation since its organization 15 years ago.

In addition to having many truck drivers on the payroll, there were several office employees. The co-op employees scheduled trucks to move the owner's products to markets in several states. Most shipments combined products produced by several of the owners.

The office employees invoiced the customers for product sales, collected the invoiced amounts, and distributed the appropriate sales proceeds to the owners. In addition, profits of the co-op were distributed as appropriate.

A co-op treasurer was responsible for the collection of monies and banking arrangements for the co-op.

One of the owner/members of the co-op became suspicious when he saw the treasurer driving a new Mercedes and showing other signs of living beyond his income.

He engaged Clyde and Chester to perform a background check on the treasurer.

Through various interviews and information obtained from public records, they found that the treasurer paid cash for the new Mercedes. He also had bought his wife a new Mercedes. In addition, the treasurer and his wife were enjoying other signs of a high living life style.

In the meantime, the treasurer had suddenly resigned from his job. Interviewing employees in the treasurer's office disclosed that the former treasurer planned to move out of state to take another job.

Concurrently, Chester discovered several irregularities in the treasurer's accounts. However, realizing that the former treasurer might soon be leaving town, they didn't have time to complete the audit review to determine the total loss before attempting to interview the former treasurer.

Under pretense, the former treasurer was called to come by the co-op office. When the former treasurer arrived, Clyde escorted him into one of the offices and confronted him with the diversion of co-op funds.

After many denials, he finally admitted that he had diverted about $1,200,000 in co-op funds to his own use.

Clipping The Co-op

Clyde obtained a signed confession from the former treasurer. In addition, Clyde was able to secure $200,000 in restitution from him.

Part of the scheme to divert funds from the co-op had been accomplished through cashing checks at local banks payable to fictitious payees.

Apparently, the treasurer had become a close personal friend of the bank tellers who did not question the treasurer's possession of checks payable to other parties.

They approached the banks for possible recoveries. Through negotiations initiated by Clyde, Chester, and the co-op's attorneys, $415,000 was recovered from the banks.

Criminal proceedings were initiated against the former treasurer.

A fidelity insurance bond claim was filed and collected covering the remaining loss of $585,000.

THE GRAPE WARS

A company owned many acres of grape vineyards in California. At harvest time, the company relied on migrant workers to pick and package the grapes.

Migrant workers and their families followed the field production cycle that began with the harvest of cabbage and asparagus in the Imperial Valley commencing at the Mexican border. The migrant workers then proceeded northward through the state to harvest carrots, onions, citrus, strawberries, nectarines, peaches, grapes, almonds, and cherries. They finally progressed northward to Oregon and Washington for the pear and apple seasons. Some migrants moved eastward to assist in the harvest of grains and cotton in the Mid-West and South.

In the summer of this particular year, Cesar Chavez, who had been trying to organize the migrant workers for several years, poised to make what appeared to be one final big effort to organize the migrant workers.

Chavez was successful in organizing a strike by the migrant workers harvesting grapes in central California. Chavez had also been successful in controlling the trucking of grapes to the packinghouses and subsequent shipments to market. This left the grape vineyard owners in a bind as the grapes would spoil if not timely harvested and shipped to market.

Although many migrant workers were convinced to strike against the growers, many others crossed the picket lines and continued to harvest grapes.

To combat this affront, Chavez organized several of his men to harass, taunt, and inflict physical harm on several of the migrant workers and their families.

The company requested Clyde and Chester investigate what was really taking place in the fields and develop some strategy to prevent the actions from accelerating into full-scale violence.

Arriving in California, they proceeded to one of the larger vineyards to observe the strike in progress. They found that there were a large number of workers in the fields harvesting grapes. However, there were a number of hecklers along the roadside with load speakers taunting the workers and making many threats.

Several Catholic Nuns were in the fields with the workers trying to see that calm prevailed.

The hecklers threats and taunts escalated until later in the day several rifles were fired into the work area. One Nun was seriously injured and several other migrant workers injured.

Clyde and Chester proceeded to plead with state and federal authorities to issue an injunction against Chavez and his union organizers. They were afraid that large-scale violence would soon break out.

While this endeavor was in progress, they discussed the trucking operation with company personnel. Considering Chavez's successes to date, it seemed like a good idea to pursue other avenues for trucking grapes to packinghouses and to market.

Although it appeared to be the lesser of two evils, it was suggested that the company make an exclusive arrangement with the Teamsters Union to provide the product transportation required. This approach met with approval.

After making arrangements with the Teamsters Union, union representatives apparently made Chavez an offer he couldn't refuse as he pulled his troops out of the fields and went back to San Diego not to be heard from in the grape fields again.

The rest of the migrant workers returned to work and the grapes were timely harvested and shipped without farther incident.

This was all accomplished before the authorities tried or were able to launch any serious action.

FARMING AND AGRICULTURE NOTES RECEIVABLE

A company was experiencing a cash crunch. It was reviewing all areas of accounts, notes receivable, and other assets that could readily be converted to cash.

The farming and agricultural division had millions of dollars in notes receivable on the books. Home office management requested Chester to review those notes held in the division office to determine their validity and that all payments due were actually current.

The majority of the notes were payable to the company by tenant farmers of Italian descent.

Chester checked all the note documents and support. He verified the notes validity by also contacting the makers of the Notes.

All payments on the notes were current. The note aging statement showed no payments were late, none even by one month. Chester verified the aging statement, note cash receipts and deposits for the last six months. Chester had never seen so much money in notes that were all that current. No irregularities were found in the notes and no fraud had occurred.

The vice president in charge of policing the notes was a six foot six man weighing 240 pounds. He was an Italian raised on the rough side of Chicago. Chester asked him how he was able to keep all those notes current. He replied, "If a payment by any person is late by a few days, I approach them with the warning to get current or today the arms, tomorrow the legs."

I guess everyone had been getting the message.

Investigating Corporate Fraud

TAMPERING WITH THE SCALES

When an almond processing plant was experiencing product shortages, Clyde and Chester were called to investigate.

The company bought almonds in the shell based on truck weights recorded by the company owned scales. The plant processed the almonds and packaged them for sale in various flavors including onion, cheese, barbeque, garlic, plain, hickory and other flavors. According to the company's purchasing, production records, inventories and product yields, the inventory records of raw almonds were overstated for the past several months.

After being told of the problem by the plant manager, Chester went outside the plant to examine the company weight scales. Chester found that the scales were built in such a way that you can move the scale weight with your finger to any weight desired.

Obviously someone involved in weighing trucks loaded with almonds from the field was reflecting a higher weight than actual. Accordingly, the company was paying for almonds not delivered.

The plant manager advised that several employees were involved in recording the truck weights as the deliveries were being made.

Clyde asked the manager to bring into the meeting room all employees that were involved in weighting trucks. At that time they had no idea who and how many employees were involved. Clyde and Chester observed the employees as they made jokes about each other and generally acting crazy. In a little while Clyde nudged Chester meaning that he had found his man. Clyde always said when he saw the guilty man the hair stood up on the back of his head. In a minute Chester picked his employee and those two were invited to two separate office rooms. In about 15 minutes they had statements from the two employees admitting they were falsifying truck weights and receiving kickbacks from the trucking firms. No other employees were involved in the fraud.

The manager was advised of their findings and of the plan to approach the trucking firms involved to recover the company's loss of about $ 50,000.

The manager told them that when you two confronted all my people and started acting like fools, I thought, "What in the world did I get myself into! Then, all of sudden you picked out two guys and left. In a few minutes it was all over. I tell you, I'll will be glad to give you the highest recommendation possible to anyone."

The manager terminated the two employees. Clyde and Chester recovered the loss from the trucking companies.

MISCELLANEOUS

AN EYE FOR A WATCH

Clyde and Chester loved to pull pranks on each other as well as others.

Clyde had a glass eye as a result of an earlier injury. On one occasion, after working a case, they got back at the home airport at mid-day. Neither of them had a car at the airport. They decided to take a taxi to the office. Their office was downtown about fifteen miles away.

Going outside to hail a taxi, they noted a young Japanese man standing in the taxi departure area. When a taxi arrived, Chester grabbed the Japanese by the arm and pushed him into the front seat of the taxi while Clyde put his suitcase in the trunk.

They got in the back seat.

The driver was the spitting image of "Rochester" who had appeared on the Jack Benny television show. He had real big eyes just like "Rochester."

Chester told the driver to take them downtown.

As they proceeded down the divided three-lane freeway, Clyde noticed that the Japanese had a beautiful, expensive, watch on his arm.

Clyde asked him how much he wanted for the watch.

The Japanese spoke very little English.

Clyde motioned at the watch on the Japanese man's arm and told him he would give him $200 for the watch.

The Japanese man shook his head no.

Clyde said, "Let me see your watch."

The Japanese, not being stupid, raised his arm to the back of the front seat to show Clyde the watch, but kept his hand around his wrist so that Clyde couldn't get the watch off his arm.

Clyde said, "I'll give you $300 for the watch."

By this time the taxi driver was getting very interested in what was going on, looking back and forth between Clyde and the young Japanese.

When the Japanese shook his head no, Clyde said, "I'll give you $400 for the watch."

When the Japanese again shook his head no, Clyde said, "I'll tell you what, I'll give you $500 and my watch for your watch."

By this time, the driver was very much involved. His eyes were as big as saucers, watching and hearing what was taking place as he drove towards downtown on the freeway.

After the Japanese shook his head no to the last offer, Clyde said, "I'll tell you what. I'll give you $500, my watch and an eye."

The Japanese man stared at him in disbelief and the taxi driver almost jumped out of his seat.

Clyde asked the Japanese which eye he wanted. When he pointed to one, Clyde popped out his glass eye and handed it to the Japanese.

The taxi driver said, "Oh my God!" and drove right into the divider fence between the north and south bound lanes on the freeway caving in the whole left side of the car.

The taxi driver then coasted off the freeway onto the shoulder area and stopped the car. The driver got out and threw all their bags on the ground, ordered them out of the taxi, and drove off.

There they were, beside the freeway, about five miles from downtown. The charade had backfired on them.

They grabbed their bags and the Japanese by the arm and walked into town to the office fully deflated by the experience.

OUTFOXING THE FOX

Private Investigators are often engaged to serve subpoenas when police or court appointed persons have failed in a reasonable time to locate and serve the named individual.

Such was the case involving a wealthy business owner in a major midwestern city who had successfully dodged several people for over a year who had tried to serve him with a subpoena.

Clyde and Chester were hired to see if they could serve a subpoena on the business owner who was involved currently in a large civil lawsuit. It was imperative that the man be served before the first of the next year.

As it was almost Christmas, not many investigators were interested in going out of town on such an endeavor.

One of the investigators working for Clyde and Chester said he would give it a try and left for Chicago.

The investigator kept surveillance on the man for a couple of days and found that there was little opportunity to get close to him as he kept a number of people around him constantly at his office on the top floor of a high rise office building in the heart of the city.

Trying to think of how he might reach the owner, the investigator studied a list of the man's clients that had been furnished prior to his trip. He hit upon an idea.

Late in the afternoon two days before Christmas, the investigator took several boxes, stuffed them with weighted materials, and wrapped the boxes with expensive Christmas paper and ribbons.

He rented a delivery uniform from a prominent local department store. He then posed as a delivery boy from that store.

The investigator, with the boxes in tow, was allowed entrance to the top floor suite of offices occupied by the man being pursued.

He approached the desk of the man's secretary stating that he had Christmas packages for the owner of the company from one of his major customers.

The secretary said she would be glad to place them in her boss's office.

The investigator advised her that he had been instructed to deliver the packages personally as they were quite valuable.

The secretary entered her boss's office and advised him of the deliveries. Greed set in and the owner invited the investigator into his office.

The investigator placed the boxes on the desk and immediately whipped out the subpoena delivering the summons.

The man cussed the investigator. Then he laughed and complimented him on his ingenuity in gaining service when no one else had been able to do so for well over a year.

Sometimes you just have to "Outfox the Fox."

THE PRE-EMPLOYEMENT PHYSICAL

One day after lunch, Chester stopped by a company's personnel department to pick up some papers. He noted that the two nurses in the department were huddled together talking frantically.

Chester asked them what had happened.

They refused to tell him. Chester insisted.

They reluctantly told Chester that a young lady had been scheduled for a company pre-employment physical exam at 11:00 am that morning.

The company doctor had called earlier and said that he wouldn't be able to give the exam until later that afternoon.

When they advised their boss, the departmental manager, he advised them not to worry. He said he would take care of it.

When the young lady came in for her physical, the boss donned a white doctor's jacket and took the woman into the exam room. He told her to disrobe and put on a smock. He then proceeded to give her a complete physical examination.

The nurses were panicked. If the woman found out she had not been examined by the company doctor, they knew she would sue and probably own the company.

Chester went to Clyde's office and told him what he had learned.

Clyde advised Chester to obtain signed written statements from the two nurses setting forth in complete detail what they had told him.

He returned to the personnel department and obtained signed statements.

Clyde took the two statements to the CEO of the company for his review.

The CEO was furious and directed that the manager of the department be terminated immediately.

The manager was terminated and the nurses sworn to secrecy about the matter.

Clyde and Chester never knew if the woman got the job.

THE LOBBYIST

The company had an office in Washington, D. C. that handled its lobbying activities. An officer of the company, an office manager, and several secretarial personnel headed the office.

Clyde and Chester flew to Washington, D. C. on a company airplane to review the office accounts relative to a suspected fraud.

In checking the office accounts, it became apparent that the office manager was receiving kickbacks from office supply companies.

Several office supply companies were confronted with the kickback suspicions. Most companies admitted giving a 10% kickback to the company's office manager that resulted in the companies overcharging the company about 20% for such supplies and equipment.

Quick calculations indicated a loss to the client of about $45,000.

The office manager was called into the office by Clyde and confronted with the information obtained. He readily admitted in a signed statement his scheme of receiving kickbacks and was terminated.

As the investigation had run into the evening, they were not sure if other employees were involved. A locksmith was called in to change out all the office door locks.

The next morning they had determined that no one else was involved. Keys were then made available to the appropriate employees.

Chester noted that the past two officers in charge of the office had become alcoholics. He asked the current officer in charge to tell him what a typical day's office activity was like in his job.

He advised Chester that a typical day of lobbying activity with the congressmen consisted generally of taking about four congressmen to breakfast where they had a few drinks each.

The officer then returned to the office for a couple hours work.

At noon he entertained several congressmen over lunch and had several drinks.

Then, it was back to the office for a couple hours. He then entertained several congressmen during the afternoon cocktail hour.

The Lobbyist

Later several were taken to dinner and drinks. Then he was expected to acquire girls for them for the rest of the evening.

The officer said he usually got home about 1 o'clock in the morning completely bombed out and of no use to his family.

He said this kind of activity went on day after day until it was no wonder the prior officers had become alcoholics. The officer said you just couldn't imagine the tickets to events, trips, and large gratuities demanded by the congressmen.

The day Clyde and Chester arrived the officer had warned them to request the company pilots take the airplane to an airport away from Washington, D. C. until they were ready to go back home. The officer said the congressmen had lookouts at the airport that would tell them of the various company airplanes in town so they could demand a ride home to their district over the weekend.

Originally, they planned on being in Washington only one day. Therefore, they didn't heed his advice.

Sure enough, on Friday morning the telephone started to ring off the hook with various congressmen demanding rides to Oklahoma City, Little Rock, Baton Rouge, Austin, etc. with a "by-the-way," we expect a ride back to Washington on Monday.

Chester called the pilots to file a flight plan for late in the afternoon. Then later change departure time for noon when they would be at the airport to leave. They left without being caught up in all the demands.

It's interesting now over 35 years later of all the self-righteous proclamations by certain congressmen who went after Clinton and others with the same charges that they also shared guilt.

Clyde and Chester always said, "Give us 30 days in rotten Washington, D. C. and we could get rid of over half the sorry, two-faced Congressmen on various violations of the law." But of course nothing like that will ever happen as Congress makes the laws and builds in the loopholes.

Investigating Corporate Fraud

WHAT HAPPENED TO THE STOCK?

Clyde and Chester were asked by the company to investigate the loss of several packages of blank company corporate stock certificates.

The investigation conducted by Clyde and Chester disclosed the following series of events.

American Bank Note Corporation located in New York City printed the company's stock certificates.

Three types of certificates were printed; 100 share certificates, less than 100 share certificates, and certificates where the number of shares were left blank. When the certificates in blank were used, the number of shares to be issued were typed in the appropriate block on the certificate and the certificate then embossed with the same number of shares.

On one occasion, the company instructed American Bank Note to ship 500 sequentially numbered blank stock certificates to The Northern Trust Company in Chicago.

A bonded carrier obtained the certificates at American Bank Note and made delivery to the air carrier at a New York City airport.

A bonded carrier picked up the package from the airline at the Chicago airport and reportedly made delivery to Northern Trust.

At each point of receipt and delivery the carrier obtained signed receipts.

About four weeks later, Northern Trust gave notification to the company that the certificates had not been received. The person in the Trust Department who presumably signed the receipt at Northern Trust upon delivery could not be identified. Apparently, this was the location where the stock certificates were stolen. The certificates were never found.

The company was requested to issue a "stop notification" on these sequentially numbered certificates to the transfer and co-transfer agents and the registrar and co-registrars of the company's common stock.

At that time none of these shares had come to the attention of the transfer agents or registrars. Should such shares eventually be tendered, they would not be accepted. Accordingly, the company would incur no loss.

What Happened To The Stock

Often when blank shares of common stock are stolen, they end up being pledged as collateral for loans from a financial institution, primarily overseas.

We can only guess at the possibility that these shares may be laying in a bank vault somewhere, possibly overseas pledged as loan collateral.

STOLEN LADIES PURSES

Women in the company were experiencing their purses being stolen during the lunch hour. A search of the trash areas at the company produced the purses but the contents had been stripped.

Clyde and Chester were called to suggest a way to stop this theft. They thought an employee of the company probably perpetrated the thefts.

Clyde obtained powder from a local bank that was used to mark their money in case of theft. When a thief handled money, his hands turned purple.

Three ladies purses were planted in obvious places during the next lunch hour with the money inside sprinkled with the powder.

Sure enough, the purses disappeared. They were found in a trash bin again but the money and credit cards were gone.

Supervisors in the building were notified to look for an employee with purple hands working in their department. The purple dye could not be washed away with soap and water.

Shortly, Clyde received a call that an employee in one of the departments came back to work after the lunch break with purple hands.

Clyde took the employee to his office and after faced with the facts, the employee signed a statement admitting his thefts. No recoveries could be obtained from the employee. He was terminated and turned over to the police.

CROSSING AGAINST THE LIGHT

One day at noon Chester left his office building to go out for lunch. As he approached the corner of the block to cross the street, the overhead stoplight turned red.

At that moment, however, a man who Chester knew started across the street against the red light. A policeman happened to be standing in the middle of the street and blew his whistle for the man to stop.

Instead of turning back, the man gave the policeman the "bird" and cursed him. He then proceeded across the street and disappeared into the crowd.

He thought the man's behavior was highly unusual and after lunch relayed what he had seen to Clyde.

Clyde told Chester that in his experience people who acted in this manner had something psychologically wrong.

On a hunch, Clyde checked local criminal records and found that this man had been arrested three times for homosexual activity in city public restrooms.

Clyde asked Chester, "Where does this man work?"

He replied, "He works in the company's treasury department handling cash receipts and deposits."

As the man worked for the company, Clyde advised that they would notify the department head of their findings and suggest that a routine audit be made of the cash receipts and deposits handled by that employee during the past year.

They made the notification and suggested an audit be conducted. A couple of weeks later, they were advised by the audit department of results of the audit. Over the past year and a half nearly $65,000 was missing from receipts handled by the man in question.

Clyde was asked to interrogate the man about the shortage.

The man finally admitted his theft and provided a detailed statement covering his fraudulent activities.

The man was married and had three children. He didn't want his family to know about his previous arrests. He stated that he stole money in order to pay for lawyers to defend him on those previous arrest charges.

Obviously, he now could no longer hide the fact from his family that he had stolen money from his employer or the prior arrests.

The man was fired and subsequently prosecuted for theft. A fidelity bond insurance claim was filed by Chester to recover the company's loss.

It always seemed ironic how little incidents like crossing the street against the light could lead to the discovery of fraud.

(Footnote: It was reported that the former employee was stabbed to death in a local bar shortly after serving his time in jail)

THE TUGBOAT COLLISION

A law firm was engaged as plaintiff's attorney in a civil suit involving the collision of two tugboats in Galveston Bay. Without service on the defendant's tugboat captain, pursuit of the plaintiff's lawsuit would be greatly handicapped.

Clyde and Chester were engaged to locate the tugboat captain and serve him with a subpoena with the objective of obtaining a deposition.

After considerable effort, Chester located the residence of the tugboat captain. The house was located in a run-down part of the city off the ship channel.

Chester made several trips to the home and either no one was at home or the captain's wife covered for her husband advising that the captain wasn't there.

He visited several of the bars in the area and found one the captain frequented. The bartender told Chester that the tugboat captain had not worked for several months. He came to the bar about noon everyday and went home by mid-afternoon in a drunken state.

Chester hung around the bar one afternoon when the captain was there. When it looked like the captain was about to leave, Chester left and drove a few houses down from the man's residence and waited for him to get home.

The tugboat captain obviously knew the law firm was trying to gain service as three or four other persons had tried to serve him unsuccessfully for several months.

When Chester saw the man go into the house, he waited about thirty minutes and went to the front door. When the tugboat captain's wife came to the front door, she denied that her husband was at home. She said she had not seen him for a week.

Chester told her that was too bad as he had a final paycheck for several thousand dollars due the captain from his last job. The wife said she would deliver it to her husband if and when he got home.

The wife was told that her husband had to sign a receipt in person in order to receive the check. Chester said he would come back again in several days when her husband might be home.

About that time Chester heard a drunken grunt from the back of the house, "Wait a minute." In a few minutes a man staggered to the front door.

Chester asked him if he was the tugboat captain and he said he was. Handing the man the envelope, Chester said, "Congratulations you have just been served a subpoena to give a deposition and appear in court."

The Tugboat Collision

Chester could hear the man cursing him all the way to his car.

After reporting to the client that service had been given on the tugboat captain, the client asked Chester to investigate the tugboat accident to see if any information could be gathered beneficial to the case.

Clyde suggested that Chester check to see if an accident report had been filed or obtained by the Coast Guard.

Chester went to the Coast Guard office just before lunch and met an officer with the Coast Guard. Chester invited him to lunch stating he would like to learn how the coast guard investigated offshore accidents. Over lunch, he learned the type of information obtained and how it was maintained in the Coast Guard files.

When they returned to the office, he asked if he could see the file relating to that particular accident he was currently investigating. The file was pulled but the coast guard officer told him he could not show him the file. He stated that he might be able to confirm some information that Chester already knew.

As Chester knew the tugboat captain was a heavy drinker, he asked if the file showed the captain to be drunk at the time of the accident. The report confirmed this to be true. Taking a stab in the dark, Chester asked if the file also showed the captain to be operating the tugboat without a pilot's license. The answer was affirmative.

Chester knew the information obtained would greatly facilitate his client. Chester asked how a copy of the file could be obtained. He was told that the information in the file could be obtained through a court subpoena.

When Chester reported his findings, the client was elated. The client advised that a subpoena would soon be obtained to get a copy of the file to verify Chester's findings.

The information obtained resulted in the client winning the civil suit against the defendant who owned the tugboat piloted by the drunken unlicensed tugboat captain.

The client was obviously pleased and the law firm gave Clyde and Chester considerable more business in the future.

UNAUTHORIZED TRIP

It seemed like over night that new foreign made adding machines began appearing in various company departments. Although the new adding machines were smaller and easier to use than the current older machines, they were still very useful and would bring very little revenue in the used machine market.

A new adding machine was put on Chester's desk without being requested or authorized. Chester decided to find out who authorized and purchased the new adding machines. No solicited bids were found nor received to establish price and quality of other competing adding machines available.

After making several inquiries, one employee in the equipment supply and repair department was found to have authorized and purchased the machines. During subsequent discussions with departmental management, Chester learned that they had just discovered that their employee was provided an all expense paid trip to Sweden to spend "two weeks" touring the company's manufacturing plant. None of his supervisors were aware nor had they authorized this trip. The employee had taken a two-week vacation in order to take the trip.

However, taking such a trip or receiving other gratuities was in violation of company policy. Whether or not purchasing the new adding machines were a good replacement or necessary for the existing machines, the employee had placed himself in a position to not only receive a once in a lifetime trip but also subsequently receive continuing improper gratuities from the manufacturing company.

These employee activities were further discussed with Company management that resulted in the immediate termination of the employee. No subsequent purchases or payments for equipment will be made without the approval at the appropriate level of management.

The recovery of any losses connected to the purchase of the new machines was limited only to the sale of the old machines.

PREVENTING ASSAULT ON A CELEBERITY

When the daughter of a world-renowned attorney broke up with her boy friend, she was scared, as he had threatened to kill her. He was especially mean when he was drunk, that was now most of the time. She was afraid he would break into her apartment and kill her. She advised her father of her fears.

Her father approached Clyde and Chester to provide his daughter with 24 hour armed protection for at least a couple of weeks. In the past they had never personally been armed, nor had their guards, when on an investigative or security assignment. However under the circumstances they agreed to accept the assignment.

They made a security review of the daughter's apartment and placed their most trusted guards at various possible entry points. Clyde and Chester also provided protection as this was a 24-hour a day job. They had all stood guard with either shotguns or pistols. This continued for a couple of weeks without incident. They hoped that the Ex had finally moved on.

They advised the attorney that it would probably be a good idea for his daughter to leave town for a little while in order for us to confirm that the Ex had given up on pursuing his daughter. He agreed and his daughter left for a short trip to Europe.

After this assignment was completed, Clyde and Chester thought about the serious consequences that could have occurred. They vowed to never take another armed assignment in the future.

SECURING $ 1,000,000 IN CASH

One of our clients supplied new automobiles from his district supply depot to various auto dealership operations in a five state area. The client wanted to do something special for the outstanding salesmen of the year at the various dealerships.

The client called Clyde and Chester advising that he was having $ 1,000,000 in cash transported that day to the well-known Shamrock Hotel in Houston to be distributed that night to the applicable salesmen that were flying to Houston for a big dinner celebration. The client wanted them to make a security review at the hotel and provide appropriate security for guarding the money from its arrival at the hotel and throughout the evening until distribution was complete.

As Clyde and Chester had a sizeable guard service at that time, they made a security review at the hotel to determine where security was necessary. Guards were assigned to designated areas to be present when the money arrived. They kept the area secure throughout the day and evening.

That evening after dinner, the client placed a large message board on one of the walls in the room. Slips of paper with various amounts of money ($ 40,000, $ 30.000, $ 20,000 etc.) had been placed in the big balloons. Each salesman was given three darts to throw at the balloons. He received the amount of money on the slip in each balloon that he popped. Clyde and Chester also assisted in the handling of the money given to the salesmen. This went on throughout the evening. When the dinner was over and the open bar closed, the salesmen returned to their rooms in the hotel that were all on the same floor. Security was provided throughout the night until the men left the next day.

Clyde and Chester were very relieved that no incident had occurred as that was a lot of responsibility. The client was very appreciative of their service and the great success of the evening affair.

CROSS-DRESSED ATTORNEY

Clyde and Chester finished a review at a produce storage and marketing operation in Southern California. The review was made because of product sales shortages. An employee was identified as working with a buyer to receive a kickback for delivering product without invoicing the buyer. The employee was interrogated by Clyde and Chester wrote out in longhand the statement covering the employee's confession. While admitting his fraudulent activity, the employee stated that he started stealing since it was well known that the plant manager and assistant manager had been stealing for sometime. Chester included this information in the employee's statement. Investigation of the manager and assistant manager's activities were placed on hold until proper management was notified of the apparent wide spread problem.

If the matter were pursued then and the manager and assistant manager of the plant were found guilty and terminated there would be no supervisory personnel left to operate the plant.

After arriving back home, Chester was summoned to the company general council's office. The attorney proceeded to chew Chester up one side and down the other stating that you never include in statements any information relating to other employee's alleged fraudulent activities. The attorney told Chester that he would never take a statement like that again.

When his ranting finally subsided, Chester told him that he might be a good corporate attorney but you don't know squat about civil and criminal law. When taking a statement covering fraud you take down everything that the person tells you. Other wise if I am on the witness stand during prosecution, the defense attorney will obviously ask if I had taken the former employees statement. I will have to reply yes. Then the prosecutor will ask if the statement included everything the employee told me. I will have to reply no. When I admit that, the prosecutor will say you just picked and chose what you wanted. What else did you leave out? I think you only put in the statement derogatory information against my client and left out other pertinent information that might be favorable to my client. The court will then be asked to throw out the statement and then the employee probably walks free. Chester told the attorney he didn't know where he got his statement but that he will continue to take statements as he had in the past.

Chester left the attorney's office angry about what had transpired, as it appeared that certain management was trying to interfere with Clyde and Chester's investigations.

When heading for an elevator Chester passed in front of a secretary he had know for many years. She asked Chester what was the matter. Chester told her of his encounter with the attorney.

She said, "Let me tell you a story about your 'favorite attorney'. Every Friday night he comes over to my apartment. He puts on my underwear, bra, blouse, skirt, sweater, slip, high heel shoes, hair combs, etc. and parades preening around in my apartment all evening pretending to be a lady." She said that since the attorney is such a big wheel in the company she didn't feel that she could do anything to stop it.

Chester told her, "Let's see if I can do something about it." Chester went to Clyde's office and told him of his encounter with the attorney and the conversation with the secretary. Chester advised that the company's top executive should be advised of this encounter. Clyde agreed and they passed on the conversations to the executive. He said he appreciated this information very much as he had been trying to justify getting rid of the attorney. The executive called the attorney to his office and terminated him immediately.

Sometimes a little revenge is sweet!

THE BOTCHED EMPLOYMENT SEARCH

When the company established a new senior executive position, a major employee search company was engaged. Descriptions of the job and the desired qualifications for the position were provided the search firm.

The search firm was instructed to present five qualified candidates to the company after proper vetting.

The company reviewed the paperwork presented by the search firm on the five best candidates according to their screening process. The search firm represented that each candidate had survived an extensive background check.

The company selected one of the candidates and prepared to offer the candidate the new senior executive position. Before making such an offer, the company CEO requested Clyde Wilson to conduct a background check on the prospective employee although the search firm represented such search had already been thoroughly conducted.

During the background check Clyde discovered that the prospective employee while driving drunk five years earlier had run over and killed a young boy. A settlement had been reached with the boy's family. Using his political contacts, the man had been able to stall criminal action for a few years until the matter finally went away. The candidate was also found to possibly be an alcoholic.

Based on Clyde's findings, the company was able to avoid a potential bad decision. Obviously, the company sought and found another major employee search firm to provide candidates for the senior executive position.

To avoid a possible repeat of this situation in the future the company requested Clyde to conduct a background check on all new potential employees.

Made in the USA
Columbia, SC
12 April 2018